"This book shows how philosophy and social science are good travel companions. Its message is neat: philosophy is the perfect schema from which to interrogate the use of concepts in management research. What is distinctive is the exploration of management and organizational philosophy from the viewpoint of those who occupy a subaltern position in power-laden arrangements."

Prof. Silvia Gherardi, *Dipartimento di Sociologia e Ricerca Sociale, University of Trento, Italy*

"I've been waiting for a book like this for all of my academic life, first as a PhD student and now as faculty who works with PhD students. At a time when management research is waking up to grand societal challenges, this engagement with philosophy may spur much-needed new directions in our field."

Suhaib Riaz, PhD, *Associate Professor of Management, Telfer School of Management, University of Ottawa, Canada*

"This book provides the essential philosophical basis to develop a package of method, theory and style for scholars who want to engage in reflexive, non-traditional organizational research. It is an invaluable guide that will not only help a new generation of management researchers but also change organizational research itself. A must-read!"

Maddy Janssens, *Professor at the Department of Work & Organisation Studies, KU Leuven, Belgium*

"Philosophy is the absent centre of management studies. It pervades all of what we think and feel and do and imagine. It tells us that 'we' is a contested notion, for in time and space ideas differ fundamentally. This book brings philosophy into its rightful position at the heart of management studies and is to be welcomed for the warm illumination that it will provide."

Gibson Burrell, *Professor of Organisation Theory, University of Leicester, UK*

"In an age where management research is increasingly judged by its social impact, it is critical that our work as scholars is built on a strong intellectual foundation. Philosophy is that foundation, and this book introduces its central tenets in an insightful, intelligent and accessible way. Highly recommended for doctoral students and early career researchers, and a timely prompt to thinking for more experienced researchers".

Carl Rhodes, *Professor of Organization Studies, University of Technology Sydney, Australia*

Philosophy and Management Studies

Irrespective of whether one thinks of philosophy explicitly, each organizational researcher is a philosopher. A philosophical position is predicated on a variety of approaches relating to ontology, epistemology, methodology, ethics, and political positions. Depending on where one stands with regard to these philosophical building blocks, their orientation may be characterized as positivist, realist, critical-realist, and constructivist, with pragmatist and political considerations weighing in as well. Also, management theories all inhabit the same spectrum of philosophical positions that enrich them and add to their relevance to the world of firms and organizations. This book provides a broad-based commentary on the terrain of philosophy as it pertains to management studies, especially for the relatively unfamiliar organizational theorist.

This book serves as a succinct overview of the field of management philosophy as well as a roadmap for those readers who wish to explore the terrain further. The book argues that all knowledge inquiry invokes philosophy and philosophical thinking, and that the artificial separation between philosophy and social science is fallacious. Just as philosophy is everywhere, so is power, and for better or worse they go hand in hand. Hence, philosophical positions are political positions. The authors do not shy from addressing the politics of their own research practice or the subjects of their inquiry.

Philosophy and Management Studies targets a new generation of management researchers, whose interest in philosophy vastly exceeds their resources to engage with it, partly because of their unfamiliarity with its often mystifying and outsider-unfriendly conventions. It seeks to bridge the chasm between interest in philosophy in organizational studies and knowledge about it. It is not for the trained philosopher or the expert, but for a relative newcomer.

Raza Mir is Professor of Management at William Paterson University, USA. He is the co-editor-in-chief of the journal *Organization*.

Michelle Greenwood is Associate Professor in the Department of Management at Monash University, Australia. She is co-editor-in-chief of the *Journal of Business Ethics*.

State of the Art in Business Research
Series Editor: Geoffrey Wood

Recent advances in theory, methods and applied knowledge (alongside structural changes in the global economic ecosystem) have presented researchers with challenges in seeking to stay abreast of their fields and navigate new scholarly terrains.

State of the Art in Business Research presents shortform books which provide an expert map to guide readers through new and rapidly evolving areas of research. Each title will provide an overview of the area, a guide to the key literature and theories and time-saving summaries of how theory interacts with practice.

As a collection, these books provide a library of theoretical and conceptual insights, and exposure to novel research tools and applied knowledge, that aid and facilitate in defining the state of the art, as a foundation stone for a new generation of research.

Public Management
A Research Overview
Tom Entwistle

Philosophy and Management Studies
A Research Overview
Raza Mir and Michelle Greenwood

Work in the Gig Economy
A Research Overview
James Duggan, Anthony McDonnell, Ultan Sherman and Ronan Carbery

For more information about this series, please visit: www.routledge.com/State-of-the-Art-in-Business-Research/book-series/START

Philosophy and Management Studies
A Research Overview

Raza Mir and Michelle Greenwood

LONDON AND NEW YORK

First published 2022
by Routledge
2 Park Square, Milton Park, Abingdon, Oxon OX14 4RN

and by Routledge
605 Third Avenue, New York, NY 10158

Routledge is an imprint of the Taylor & Francis Group, an informa business

© 2022 Raza Mir and Michelle Greenwood

The right of Raza Mir and Michelle Greenwood to be identified as authors of this work has been asserted by them in accordance with sections 77 and 78 of the Copyright, Designs and Patents Act 1988.

All rights reserved. No part of this book may be reprinted or reproduced or utilised in any form or by any electronic, mechanical, or other means, now known or hereafter invented, including photocopying and recording, or in any information storage or retrieval system, without permission in writing from the publishers.

Trademark notice: Product or corporate names may be trademarks or registered trademarks, and are used only for identification and explanation without intent to infringe.

British Library Cataloguing-in-Publication Data
A catalogue record for this book is available from the British Library

Library of Congress Cataloging-in-Publication Data
Names: Mir, Raza A., author. | Greenwood, Michelle, author.
Title: Philosophy and management studies : a research
overview / Raza Mir and Michelle Greenwood.
Description: Abingdon, Oxon ; New York, NY : Routledge, 2022. |
Series: State of the art in business research |
Includes bibliographical references and index.
Identifiers: LCCN 2021013047 (print) | LCCN 2021013048 (ebook) |
Subjects: LCSH: Management–Philosophy. | Organization–Philosophy.
Classification: LCC HD30.19 .M57 2022 (print) |
LCC HD30.19 (ebook) | DDC 658.001–dc23
LC record available at https://lccn.loc.gov/2021013047
LC ebook record available at https://lccn.loc.gov/2021013048

ISBN: 978-1-138-49236-3 (hbk)
ISBN: 978-1-032-07363-7 (pbk)
ISBN: 978-1-351-03070-0 (ebk)

DOI: 10.4324/9781351030700

Typeset in Times New Roman
by Newgen Publishing UK

To my mother Zakia, my first teacher.
Raza Mir
To my mother, in honour of all you have given.
Michelle Greenwood

Contents

Preface   xi

1   Everyone is a philosopher   1
  Introduction 1
  Why do management researchers need philosophy? 2
  What is philosophy? 5
  Foundations of management philosophy 5
    Ontology 6
    Epistemology 7
    Methodology 9
    Ethics 10
  Philosophical worldviews 12
    Positivism 12
    Realism 13
    Critical realism 14
    Constructivism 15
    Pragmatism 16
    The political dimension 17
    Summing up 19
  Philosophy and organizational theories 19
    Positivism in strategic management 21
    Realism in strategic management 22
    Constructivism in strategic management 23
  Conclusion 24

2   Interrogating concepts   31
  Introduction 31
  Concepts as creative and reductive: addressing the nature and purposes of concepts 32
    Concepts in philosophy and social science 32

x   *Contents*

      Concepts as abstraction and classification 34
      Concepts as thick and thin 37
      The politics of thickening and thinning of concepts 38
   Concepts as commodities: addressing the thinning of concepts in management studies 39
      Concepts as fashion in management studies 39
      Two examples of concept use in management studies 42
        Justice for justice 42
        Whose culture is it anyway? 43
      The politics of thinning of concepts in management studies 45
   Concept as method: addressing the enriching of method with concepts 46
      Using 'concept as method' to problematize qualitative research 46
      Three provocations to qualitative inquiry 48
        Method without rules or goals: implications for thinking 48
        Method without subjects: implications for interviewing 51
        Method without a field: implications for studying cases 52
      The politics of 'concept as method' in management studies 54
   Conclusion 56

3 Philosophy from below   64
   The philosophy of class conflict 66
   Changing the subject: the case of feminist philosophy 68
   Postcoloniality as a case of critical constructivism 70
      Orientalism 74
      Hybridity 75
      Strategic essentialism 77
   Neo-Gramscian philosophy: subaltern studies 79
   An exemplar of critical realism: political society 81
   Reflexive ontology: the case of critical transnationalism 84
   Conclusion 88

4 The road ahead for management and organizational philosophy   97

   Index   101

Preface

In August 2020, the Academy of Management meetings were conducted online. Our Professional Development Workshop titled 'Philosophical Foundations of Organizational Research' was scheduled at the unearthly hour of 8 pm EST, which would be the dead of the night in Europe. We resigned ourselves to a sparse attendance.

Much to our astonishment, the workshop was not only very well attended, but also the enthusiasm of the attendees was undiminished by the odd time. Participants logged in from all parts of the world. They engaged animatedly with our presentations, which track closely to many of the topics we have presented in this book. They exhibited genuine interest in a philosophical approach to organizational research, though their understanding of philosophy traversed the spectrum from familiarity to relative ignorance. Many of the attendees, it turned out, were doctoral students, who were mostly from traditional institutions, pursuing traditional PhDs using traditional methodologies. They had not been exposed to a formal study of philosophy or philosophy of science in their doctoral programs. They felt alienated in their departments precisely because of their philosophical orientation, which had often been derided explicitly and implicitly by their superiors as a waste of time, and worse, as a reason why the field of management, unlike the natural sciences or even economics, lacked unified protocols of sequential knowledge-building and as a result struggled for legitimacy.

We ended the workshop with a long session where we gave the participants an opportunity to describe how they felt in the course of their doctoral careers. The scenario that emerged has strengthened our feeling that we absolutely need a variety of fora where we discuss the philosophical foundations of organizational research. The students we met at that workshop, who labored alone in programs that did not value this sort of introspection, indicated clearly to us that this was a genuine need. This was especially true of those participants who implicitly and instinctively rejected positivist modes of inquiry, and tended to be more interpretivist in their epistemological positions, even though they lacked the language to state it in those terms.

Our experience in the 2020 workshop mirrors what we had observed in workshops past; the interest in philosophy in our field vastly outstrips the resources we seem to offer. This lack emerges from a variety of institutional and structural boundary conditions. Doctoral programs across the US in particular have 'trimmed the fat' in their coursework by eliminating courses that do not deal directly with specific subfields of the area under study or with directive research methods. In the absence of any reflexivity at the program level the hierarchies within departments tend to get heightened. Each department often has its own range of 'desirable' topics where research is encouraged, and different senior faculty members lead their wards down the path of research, advising them of the topics to study, the 'gaps' to fill, the methods to adopt, and the outlets for publication. Ironically, students who enter the world of academia to escape the stultifying atmosphere of corporations find themselves exchanging one orthodoxy for another, often inflected with even more oppressive intellectual hierarchies.

It is not for us to lament, or even reflect upon, the reasons why doctoral programs in our field have chosen to excise courses that teach philosophy to incoming PhD students. The exigencies of the academic labor market, the isomorphic pulls toward a mainstream, the emerging self-fulfilling prophesies of what constitutes theory building and theory testing, who gets to be designated as a boundary pusher and what dues need to be paid before one ventures divergent opinions, these are institutionalized discussions. To question them means placing oneself outside the discourse. But one thing is certain. The ideological attempt to minimize the importance of philosophy in our field can produce dominance, but not hegemony. There will always be students who will wonder about the shifting meaning of research topics, about the nature of the reality they explore, and the fundamental assumptions that underlie their inquiry. They will question the morality of their work, and their choice of methodological tools. And we hope that if they read this book, they will find that such questions connect them to a long tradition of philosophical inquiry, which is entirely relevant to a research program in the management.

This book does not make a claim that it is novel or path-breaking. The philosophical foundations of organizational research have been covered in a large number of books and papers. We refer to several such expositions in the pages that follow. By way of making a case for this one, we contend that our book targets a new generation, whose interest in philosophy vastly exceeds their ability to engage with it, partly because of their unfamiliarity with its often mystifying and outsider-unfriendly conventions. It seeks to bridge the chasm between interest in philosophy in organizational studies and knowledge about it. We have not written this book for the philosopher or the expert, but for a relative newcomer. Our hope is that we have not fatally traded depth for simplicity.

The rest of the book comprises three chapters and a brief conclusion. The first chapter reviews various elements of the *discipline of philosophy*, especially as they relate to organizations. We believe that the *discipline of management*[1] is characterized by the understanding that the firm or the organization is a relevant unit of analysis. That unit interacts with a variety of macro-institutions (the economy, the society, the culture, the nation) as well as micro-units (individual psychology, microeconomic preferences) and engages with an infinity of social processes (technologies, communications, visuals) to produce knowledge structures that imbue our research with relevance and legitimacy. Within this framework, the first chapter provides an introduction to various elements of philosophy, highlights different positions that researchers and practitioners can take, and the different theories in our field and their philosophical underpinnings.

We begin by identifying how philosophy has been deployed in management theory, and contend that it has been present as long as the field has existed. We then introduce some of the building blocks of philosophy such as the concepts of ontology, epistemology, ethics, and methodology, and link them to issues of politics and power, thereby building what we feel is a natural bridge between philosophy and social theory.

The second chapter delves into the very knowledge structures that build, direct, and legitimatize our research, namely concepts. We explore *the concept of concepts*. Concepts are everywhere in philosophy; indeed some would go as far as to say that concepts and their creation constitute philosophy. We explore the role of concepts in philosophy, their potentiality for lofty abstraction and reductive categorization, and propose what makes for good and bad concepts. We then explore how concepts have been used and abused in management studies through the thinning and marketization of concepts. As examples, we discuss the injustices perpetrated on the concept of justice and the translation of culture from anthropological inquiry to management consultants' tool. We then introduce a twist on the concept of concepts by considering concept as method. The idea that concepts are not just interrelated to methods but are one in the same is used as provocation for rethinking our commitments in qualitative methods.

In our third chapter, we examine *philosophy from below*. We contend that mainstream discussions on philosophy have been predicated upon a variety of referents, each of which places its 'other' in the shadows. The male referent suppresses female subjectivity, the economic elite denies the subjectivity of exploited labor, whiteness defines people of color on their terms, heteronormativity denies agency to queer subjects and so forth. Such approaches may be deemed *ideological,* in that they universalize from the interests of the dominant to imply the interests of the whole. In a counter-ideological move, our approach in this chapter is not just to call out such practices but also to suggest ways in which a new philosophy can be produced, one where hitherto dominated subjectivities have free reign to engage with the world, contesting implicit referents. Marxist theory, for example, legitimizes the concerns of exploited labor, feminist theory honors the female subject, queer theory decenters heteronormativity, and postcolonial theory gives agency back to the ruled subjects of colonial practice. Our aim in this chapter is to give these groups the dignity of theory, rescuing them from the representation of their selves as existing within the realm of *culture.*

We conclude with a short chapter that provides some suggestions for taking philosophical ideas forward in management studies. At the end of the book there is an index, which is somewhat unlike other indexes. We formulated the index ourselves by hand selecting and linking concepts, authors, and works of scholarship. Thus, our index offers not just points of entry to the text but also a snapshot of our arguments and a window into our priorities.

Despite dealing with a variety of serious and theoretically dense subjects, our book has been written as a beginner-friendly tract. We hope that not only PhD students and their supervisors but also researchers at any career level who are frustrated by the spinning wheel of publishing for the sake of publishing or are just feeling a yearning in their heart of hearts will find some spark of joy or redemption in our musings. We thank our workshop participants for giving us a greater understanding of the target readership of the book. If their genuine and heartfelt desire for an introduction to philosophy is fulfilled even in small measure by this book, we will consider ourselves successful.

Note

1 We refer here to the discipline of management in a broad sense to include the study of management and organizations. Hence, throughout this book, we use the terms 'organization studies' and 'management studies' (similarly 'organization theory' and 'management theory') interchangeably. We believe that while there might be cause to see these terms differently, such differences are not relevant to our arguments.

1 Everyone is a philosopher

Introduction

Philosophy is everywhere and

> ...everyone is a philosopher, though in [their] own way and unconsciously, since even in the slightest manifestation of any intellectual activity whatever, in "language", there is contained a specific conception of the world.
>
> (Antonio Gramsci, 1971: 323)

Interest in philosophy has been an on-going feature of management research and pedagogy. Philosophy-themed books in the field of management continue to be bestsellers, while papers in peer-reviewed journals on philosophical issues continue to be heavily cited. Most books on organizational philosophy however tend to be long and dense, and are intimidating to beginners. We too have produced such a volume in the past. Indeed, this book owes its existence to the earlier publication of our co-edited volume, the *Routledge Companion to Philosophy in Organization Studies* (Mir, Willmott, & Greenwood, 2016). Like earlier volumes on organizational philosophy, ours was heavy tome. With the greatest of difficulties, we kept its size down to 350,000 words, hectoring our 60+ contributors to cut down their insights, often to 6,000 words a chapter.

In this book, we have chosen to do the opposite, and hew in the direction of brevity. We wish to distil our understanding of management philosophy in a relatively short volume, sacrificing depth for breadth, but hopefully serving as a succinct overview of the field of management philosophy as well as a roadmap for those readers who wish to explore the terrain further.

DOI: 10.4324/9781351030700-1

Why do management researchers need philosophy?

The first question that an introductory text on management philosophy needs to answer is, *do management researchers need (to study) philosophy?* The answer in our mind is a resounding yes, for three reasons.

First, whether we like it or not, we inhabit a philosophical position whenever we conduct or engage with research. When we use return-on-equity as a proxy for organizational performance (Bierly & Chakrabarti, 1996), make a case that a Likert scale, which is an interval scale, can be deployed as a ratio scale in statistical analyses (Churchill, 1979), use demographics as a basis to understand leadership behavior (Hambrick & Mason, 1984), or make a case that managerial strategy focuses on deskilling workers as a mode of control (Rowlinson & Hassard, 1994), a philosophical position underlies our contentions and our decisions, which would be worthwhile for us to make transparent.

Our field seems a bit shy to embrace a philosophical orientation. It was not always this way, as we have recalled earlier, *The Journal of the Academy of Management*, the first scholarly journal of our field featured in each of its first three volumes at least one article that overtly dealt with philosophy (Mir, Willmott, & Greenwood, 2016: 1). Perhaps the problem lies in a sense of defensiveness that emerged a few decades later. One recalls that in the 1990s, there were leaders in the Academy of Management, who panicked that we were missing the boat and at risk of disregarding a trend that might have led to the emergence of something akin to Nobel Prize in Management. For such theorists, an engagement with needless abstraction was a recipe for irrelevance. Instead, they felt that the field needed to focus on the application of disciplinarily accepted and agreed-upon assumptions, each theorist building upon the work of past stalwarts into a daisy-chain of applicable achievement, without the encumbrance of "values that emphasize representativeness, inclusiveness, and theoretical and methodological diversity" (Pfeffer, 1993: 599). Such values were to be avoided because they produced naught but negative "consequences for the field's ability to make scientific progress, which almost requires some level of consensus, as well as for its likely ability to compete successfully with adjacent social sciences such as economics in the contest for resources" (ibid: 599). The scholars who wished to impose such consensus on the field decried needless paradigm-infused chatter that it 'fragmented' the discipline with ideas that "share(d) an anti-management quality, painting managers in an increasingly negative light" (Donaldson, 1995: 1).

Such calls for paradigmatic unity were vigorously contested. Ironically, the stated demands for a tightly knit approach to organizational research such as those articulated by Pfeffer and Donaldson had the exact opposite effect, spurring a debate that underscored the importance of paradigmatic diversity in the field (Perrow, 1994; Sutton & Staw, 1995; Weick, 1995). For an entire decade and more, we debated what constituted theory and how bad theory made good research impossible (Ghoshal, 2005). If the discussion has abated somewhat, it is perhaps because of sheer fatigue on all sides. But in the end, one consensus has emerged; philosophy has a huge role to play in settling debates about truth claims, about the predictive validity of various theories, and whether our field has any relevance in an era of increasing inequality and oligopolistic corporations running roughshod over archaic systems of governance. At times, it appears that all that stands between management theory and irrelevance is philosophy.

Our second point is that the articulation of a philosophical position often helps us explain our research in ways that readers and subsequent researchers will be able to understand, follow, extend, critique, and refute (Mir & Watson, 2001). It helps us move past unfalsifiable tautologies and untestable generalizations into the realm of actionable and contestable. When theorists make truth claims about organizational actions, it is important to evaluate their implicit assumptions. The debate that follows is often very productive for both sides.

Consider, for example, an influential theory such as transaction cost economics. This theory became hegemonic in the field of management, in particular for its contention that contracts were the primary economic institutions of capitalism (Williamson, 1985). Purveyors of the theory sought to cast its conclusion in 'value-free' terms, implying that the decision between using outside contractors for economic activity (markets) and internalizing such activities within the boundaries of organizations (hierarchies) was only dictated by efficiency considerations like 'asset specificity' and 'bounded rationality,' and that a firm could only be understood as a nexus of contracts, without the need of other values such as cooperative spirit or power politics.

Economist critics of the theory found the transaction cost hypotheses to be reductive and castigated it as the latest ploy by organizational elites to justify anti-competitive expansion by firms without the encumbrance of social and government oversight (Kaufman, Zacharias, & Karson, 1995). Firms could be seen, they argued, as vehicles to create monopoly power, and to band the power of the capitalist tightly, while reducing the power of labor to negotiate collectively.

The debate however became a lot richer when it moved from the economic to the philosophical plane, when its partisans and interlocutors began to articulate and defend their philosophical positions. Some critics of the transaction cost theory accused its adherents of hiding their implicit assumptions (Ghoshal & Moran, 1996), suggesting that once their assumptions were made explicit, people would understand that it was empty of any insight. The purveyors of the theory were forced to settle the matter in the philosophical realm as well (Williamson, 1996), arguing that they were not amoral automatons, and that even though they did not deploy morality as a construct in their models, the outcome of these economic activity was not incompatible with social welfare. Whatever be the outcome, the debate itself enriched our understanding, and helped those of us at the sidelines make up our minds. Philosophy enlightens, even in the dry world of economics.

Finally, the study of philosophy in and of itself allows us to understand organizations better, link them to broader social, economic, political, and cultural institutions, and advances our understanding of working life. In its best version, it allows us to decenter the status quo, expose elitist ideologies, honor the contributions of those whose labor produces social value, and contest the modes of accumulation that destroy the planet and immiserize the working poor. When multinational corporations seek to privatize public property in the name of efficiencies, the first thing they do is to co-opt potential adversaries (like national governments) through illiberal inducements. It then becomes important and indeed incumbent upon theorists to produce an alternative philosophy that delegitimizes these practices and honors those who contest their own dispossession through acts of resistance (Banerjee, 2000).

Likewise, a philosophical orientation is needed to delegitimize research that hides ideology within its platitudes. Many times, researchers may use normative language to define a problem, thus rendering the problem statement unfalsifiable. For example, one could say, "If all employees in a firm work selflessly, performance will improve." Clearly, such a statement is not empirically researchable. A surprising number of research projects in our field do get away with such approaches, often through the creation of spurious proxies for unfalsifiable terminology (perhaps, in this case, through the representation of some construct as a stand-in for 'selflessness'). One very important element of falsifiability also includes the articulation of fundamental assumptions that underpin the research. Research that does not clarify its assumptions also runs the risk of becoming ideological, or a vehicle to universalize the interests of a small subgroup in the organizational realm (say, top managers) as the interest of the whole.

What is philosophy?

The second question we need to deal with is, *what is philosophy?* The answer to this question can be as complex as we choose to make it. Definitions are in themselves artifacts of organizational process and are ripe with implicit assumptions and accompanying ideologies. Who gets to define and how something is defined implicate our knowledge and accompanying power arrangements. Hence, throughout this volume we assume that the defining of philosophy is open and on-going, a work in progress during which we pause at any particular moment to rest on a definition that is most useful at that time in that context. For the purposes of this discussion, we start with a draft definition of philosophy as an inquiry into certain basic questions about the nature of reality, of knowledge, and the way it is acquired, of reason, of language and of morals, and of ethics and values. Implicit in this definition is the belief that philosophy is not just a matter of identifying the nature of things but also an examination of the way the world is ordered. To that end, it incorporates issues relating to politics, conflict, and change. We feel that an effective philosophical position incorporates an examination of social theory as well. To deny such an intertwining between knowledge and society is an act of social construction that is neither credible nor productive; indeed the connectedness between philosophy and social theory is a theme that will be explored throughout this volume. Hence, we view Karl Marx and Max Weber, Emile Durkheim and Sigmund Freud, Franz Fanon and Judith Butler, Michel Foucault and Gayatri Spivak, Mohandas Gandhi and WEB DuBois as philosophers. To that extent this book exhibits a somewhat eclectic approach to philosophy.

In the rest of this chapter, we outline a philosophical position keeping management and organizational theory at the forefront of our discussion. While our main focus is on the *foundations* of management philosophy, we also discuss its manifestation in various management *theories*.

Foundations of management philosophy

When we discuss the foundations of organizational philosophy, we are essentially referring to "the assumptions that underpin any truth claim and then are disrupted through their denial and the identification of the absent alternatives whose articulation produces an alternative rendition of reality" (Duberley & Johnson, 2016: 77). These assumptions relate to how we experience and know the world foremost as humans but also as researchers.

Four elements are essential to any foundational discussion of philosophy: *ontology*, *epistemology*, *methodology*, and *ethics*. Ontology refers to the nature of reality, epistemology to the nature of knowledge, methodology to the manner in which inquiry is carried out, and ethics to the moral positions that organizational actors and researchers assume, and should make explicit in their work. When researchers analyze organizations, their assumptions, their methodological choices, and even their writing style can be seen as a function of their epistemological and ontological orientation rather than a mere choice of techniques (Morgan & Smircich, 1980). Ways of thinking underlay methodologies, and the philosophical and political attitudes held by researchers determine their approach to the definition, analysis, and explication of socio-organizational issues (Burrell & Morgan, 1979).

While a detailed discussion of the philosophical foundations of management research is beyond the scope of our discussion, we would like to make a few observations about certain concepts that animate discussions of research in general. The purpose here is not so much to explain these concepts as it is to ask for a greater level of transparency on the part of researchers in examining the philosophical assumptions that underpin their research.

Ontology

Are researchers nothing more than archaeologists, sifting through rubble to find nuggets of reality? Or are they craftspeople, using various pieces to create contingent structures? Do constructs (such as market share or firm performance) exist independently of our research? Such questions are in the realm of the ontological, and are extremely relevant to organizational theory (see Al-Amoudi & Mahoney, 2016, for a succinct analysis). If one visualizes a road in a desert, it seems as if it is the best way to go from one town to another. But one can visualize a point in the past when there was no road, and indeed, when there were no towns. Likewise, in the economic realm, we can visualize a landscape before there were firms, before many of the managerial and organizational constructs that we use existed. Did we discover them, or did we invent them?

To understand the application of ontology in organizational studies, let us consider the case of institutional theory. Edwards (2016: 125–137) analyzes a variety of ontological debates that enlivened theorists' understanding of what institutions are, how they emerge, how they are sustained, and how they transform. An institution may be defined broadly as a social pattern that owes its survival to it being constantly practiced, and accepted as important and useful (Jepperson, 1991). While it initially emerges out of need, and out of the prodding of those who exercise power, it eventually acquires a legitimacy of its own, emerging as a social 'truth.' In fact, once a practice of a set of practices is ordained as an institution, it acquires the status of a 'rational myth' (Meyer & Rowan, 1991), generating its own logic as it proceeds.

Some theorists might argue that institutions are immutable entities that are discovered by theorists through research. Others might argue that institutions emerge from the interplay of human volition and constraining structures. The interlinked structures that produce organizational institutions include not just an organizational context, but also from broader contexts such as national systems, sectoral effects, and other external factors. Other theorists might see a display of power and privilege by elite actors in fashioning macro-institutional climates. For example, organizational logics could be influenced by international regimes like the World Bank, International Monetary Fund, and the World Trade Organization that push toward an institutional climate characterized by intellectual property rights protection, the use of information technology networks to provide accountability and modernization. National economic agendas, academic scholars, and practitioners would all form the building blocks of the institutional matrix. Technological symbols like information and communication technology would be symbolically deployed by those in power to push their agenda for change within economies, nations, and corporations.

The issue at hand is simple. Are we cartographers mapping organizational reality, or are we explorers walking on virgin terrain, creating a path with our footsteps for other lost souls to follow, producing a road over time? Does the truth lie somewhere in the middle? Like the 'free will vs. determinism' debate in traditional philosophy, positions on organizational ontology traverse a spectrum. Our understanding of ontology, as we explain later, is one of the fundamental building blocks of whether we describe ourselves as positivists, realists, critical realists, constructivists, and pragmatists. This has profound effect on how we do our research and how we represent our findings.

Epistemology

The clarification of *epistemological* assumptions is equally important. For example, how did management researchers agree (for the most part) that analytical statistics involving regression and analysis and representation of data and findings in a particular way would be considered 'knowledge?' Clearly, we were following other social sciences such as sociology and economics along that path. Over time, we have 'learned' a few things. Large samples. Analytical over descriptive statistics. Developing a literature review for our papers, identifying a gap in the existing knowledge that our work will fill. These are the building blocks of our epistemology.

Perhaps the origin of this collective understanding of what constitutes knowledge can be traced to the 'Vienna Circle,' a group of logical empiricists that were formed in the first part of the twentieth century, which formalized the laws that we now know by the term 'logical positivism.' Driven by a sense of natural science envy, the Vienna Circle sought to find natural progressions in social phenomena. In their desire to create binaries and hierarchies, they privileged *erklären* (the search for a causal explanation for phenomena) over *verstehen* (a more interpretive understanding) (Uebel, 2012). Influential reports into 'the business school' in 1959 by the Ford Foundation and Carnegie Corporation advanced the dominance of quantitative research in research training, and influenced the Academy of Management to claim 'controlled objective research' as essential for research standards and disciplinary legitimacy (Zyphur & Pierides, 2020: 12). Eventually, management studies like other social sciences began to be dominated by a 'statistical turn,' whereby descriptive statistics were considered inferior, and the active manipulation of large sample data through increasingly sophisticated statistical methods became a marker of legitimacy. 'Qualitative research' emerged as a term that described all modes of inquiry that did not deploy analytic statistics, and often carried with it the stigma of illegitimacy. In a world dominated by patriarchy, qualitative research was also *feminized* (Acker, 2000).

As Scherer, Does and Marti (2016: 33–50) discuss in their synthesis of epistemological approaches to organizational theory, the idea that knowledge is 'justified true belief' emerged from Plato. But which 'belief' gets to be cast as 'knowledge' is what needs to be unpacked epistemologically. 'Justification' is the building block of epistemology. When we develop constructs such as 'reliability' and 'validity' in our research methods, we are staking out epistemological positions. Other epistemological positions include what can be treated as 'evidence' in research settings, whether the knowledge we accrue is considered value-free or contextual and value laden, and what is a subject–object relation. If we believe that human beings (say managers) produce organizational outcomes (say performance), then we are saying that managers are subjects and performance is the object. In other situations, the economic context might be considered powerful enough to influence human behavior, in which case the subject–object relationship is reversed.

Such questions track closely to the ontological issues we discussed earlier. Can we think of researchers as simply highlighting what already exists? Or do people create things as they go along? For example, in its October 2020 lawsuit against Google, the US Department of Justice observed that it held 92% of the market for internet search, which it termed socially unproductive. Such a statement is easy to understand for us in 2021. But in 1990, the concept of a market for internet search would be meaningless. Google has argued that even in 2021, this concept is meaningless, because internet searches are one of several ways in which humans gather information (apps, visual data, oral communication, etc.). The definition of a 'market for search,' they contend, is therefore meaningless. Moreover, they argue that new modes of inquiry are emerging, which we cannot even visualize. Is 'the market for internet search' a 'justified true belief,' or has it been produced as a result of our inquiry? If organizations create industries and products, do they also fashion their own knowledge as well? Do researchers do the same?

Linking the above paragraph to the discussion on ontology, we can see that ontological and epistemological assumptions tend to be correlated. To that extent, philosophical positions often come with closely banded ontological and epistemological assumptions.

Methodology

Researchers must also analyze the much used but rarely understood concept of *methodology*. The term *methodology* is much broader than mere *method*, the important 'ology' (meaning 'study or science of' in Greek) often being overlooked. A method is a tool or a technique that is used in the process of inquiry. However, methodology is an inquiry into the process of inquiry. Thus, methodology needs to be used specifically, as a way to express an "intricate set of ontological and epistemological assumptions that a researcher brings to his or her work" (Prasad, 1997: 2). Methodological approaches are closely associated therefore with ontological and epistemological positions, as well as ways in which researchers plan to bring *rigor* to theory research, and the analytical approaches they bring to bear in the analysis of their data. It is here that researchers need to develop their own standards of what constitutes rigorous research in specific methodological traditions.

In their analysis of methodology as it pertains to organizational philosophy, Joanne Duberley and Phil Johnson develop this concept further, linking methodology to the theoretical positioning of researchers, the relationship between a philosophical position adopted and research methods used, strategies used by researchers to establish and communicate rigor, and the analytical lenses through which researchers examine their data (Duberley & Johnson, 2016: 67). The methodological approach used by researchers can be placed on a continuum, rather than in watertight compartments. On one end of this spectrum, we may place those traditions that focus on the 'discovery of the exogenous world,' and on the other end, those that study the 'fashioning of the subject of inquiry.'

Perhaps it is important at this juncture to address the issue of qualitative and quantitative research, a binary that, despite our protestation to the contrary, we must accept has been foisted on us (Mir, 2018). It is perhaps very instructive to realize that, by the yardsticks used by social science research of the twenty-first century, Charles Darwin, Karl Marx, and Sigmund Freud would be considered 'qualitative researchers.' While that is impressive company indeed, it highlights the fact that the binary division of empirical social science research into sealed boxes named 'qualitative' and 'quantitative' is an act of discursive violence. "We must not imagine," Michel Foucault had declared in his essay *The Order of Discourse*, "that the world turns towards us a legible face, which we would have only to decipher; the world is not the accomplice of our knowledge; there is no prediscursive providence that disposes the world in our favor." In his ringing words, "we must conceive analysis as a violence we do to things, or in any case as a practice that we impose upon them" (Foucault, 1983: 127).

Often, the research traditions of our field succumb to the temptation to evaluate research according to templates that have been developed for other traditions. It is tiresome for interpretive researchers to encounter queries about reliability and validity from journal reviewers. Ethnographers are tripped up about issues of 'generalizability,' while issues of 'falsifiability' are directed against hermeneuticians. One political question that continues to animate research in the social sciences relates not to higher order constructs like 'wisdom,' 'knowledge,' or even 'information,' but that lowly term 'data.' What constitutes data in social environments where the signal-to-noise ratio is way lower than in the neater laboratories that cause us to (misinformedly) envy our counterparts in the natural sciences? We may have finally declared an uneasy truce in the methodology wars between the qualitative and quantitative approaches, but this has largely been at the expense of the quantification of qualitative methods. Thus debates about the legitimacy of what constitutes 'data' have continued to rage in a variety of spheres.

Ethics

The issue of ethics and ethical discourses in the world of organizational theory has been a fraught one. Edward Wray-Bliss implicitly argues for an ambivalent, even a suspicious attitude to it (Wray-Bliss, 2016: 51–65). We agree with that position. While ethical considerations are paramount in organizational research, we need to debunk the narrow understanding of ethics as 'following rules.' Ethics is not just about protection of the individual subject of our research, but represents a broader concern for a collective subject, imbued in traditions of resistance and emancipation (Greenwood, 2016). Ethics implies ensuring that our work is not deployed to protect the powerful at the expense of the oppressed, or to naturalize power relations as normal or normative. Sometimes, resistance is the most ethical option, both for us as researchers and for the subjects we study.

Likewise, issues such as gaining access, transparency of objectives, and ways in which research findings will be shared with informants constitute an important element of ethics. Of course, the issue of ethics carries its own set of ambivalences. Some of the best research has been carried out surreptitiously. For example Upton Sinclair, the muckraking journalist, conducted a stealthy study of the conditions under which laborers worked in the meat packing industry in the USA at the turn of the twentieth century. Had he not done so, there would not have been the public furor that his findings created (interestingly presented not as a scholarly or journalistic piece, but as fiction in his 1906 novel *The Jungle*) that eventually led to the Pure Food and Drug Act and the Meat Inspection Act (Barkan, 1985). Yet, Sinclair's work like so many influential academic researchers from the twentieth century (Phillip Zimbardo, Stanley Milgram, and Erving Goffman) would be stopped in their tracks by the institutional review boards of our era, research ethics committees established to purportedly safeguard the very populations that such research might liberate (Greenwood, 2016).

On the other hand, many researchers who imbed themselves in organizations do so with the tacit approval of top management, and may provide pointlessly hagiographic accounts of those firms, which are later shown to be corrupt (Rishi & Singh, 2011). Indeed, the issue of ethics is fraught, but it is extremely important for researchers to be cognizant of the ethical implications of their research beyond the research process. Focusing on procedural issues such as permissions, informed consent, and data storage reduces ethics to a tick box compliance exercise at the expense of the ethical import of the whole knowledge creation project. By not considering the ethical implications of the purpose and outcomes of their research, management scholars risk being criticized for carrying the water for corporate elites at the expense of labor, the environment, and disadvantaged stakeholders. For example, the construct of corporate social responsibility has been misused to advocate for lesser oversight of corporations by society, and as a legitimizer for an corporation's relentless pursuit of value, at the expense of other marginalized social actors (Marens, 2010).

Philosophical worldviews

A further taxonomy is important here. Philosophical inquiry is premised upon a variety of broad philosophical assumptions, which good thinkers need to make transparent in their work. As indicated our positions with regard to ontology, epistemology, methodology, and ethics are inextricably related and indicative of an overall worldview or paradigm. The term *paradigm* is understood here as defined by Burrell and Morgan (1979: 23, 36) as a set of "meta-theoretical assumptions which understate the frame of reference, mode of theorizing and modus operandi of social theorist who operate within them," a broader idea than intended by Kuhn (1970). Such assumptions may be broadly classified as positivism (Schlick, 1991), realism (Leplin, 1984), critical realism (Bhaskar, 1978), and constructivism (Von Glaserfield, 1995). The four philosophical positions are closely interlinked with the ontological and epistemological positions that researcher bring to bear in their work. As with all categorizations of social phenomenon, the worldviews we depict here are socially constructed; this means that as a minimum they should be understood as having fuzzy boundaries and existing on a spectrum,

Two further dimensions may be added, pragmatism and the political perspective. Pragmatism attempts to shift philosophy into the dimension of the *possible*, arguing that a philosophical position must primarily be actionable. In a different vein, the political position suggests that no philosophical position is complete unless it examines the sociopolitical status quo and subjects it to scrutiny.

Positivism

Positivism is premised on the pre-eminence of *observability* in inquiry. Proposed in the eighteenth century by the French philosopher Auguste Comte, positivism is founded on the idea that the human mind, progressing from spirituality and metaphysics, achieves certitude by understanding the laws that underlie phenomena. Comte's ideas recommended that the scientific approaches adopted in mathematics and the natural sciences should be adopted in social sciences as well.

A positivist approach to management and organizational theory was heralded by the research of Frederick Taylor conducted at the turn of the century that led to the publication of his celebrated book *The Principles of Scientific Management* (Taylor, 1911). Taylor had argued that accurate measurements of work processes needed to become the basis for crafting and executing strategy. Subsequent research works in production technology, information systems, finance, and other fields owe much to the principles of positivism and continue to be deployed extensively by researchers and practitioners in devising 'optimal' practices (O'Connor, 1989).

Other great proponents of positivism in organizational research include the researchers who designed the Hawthorne studies. Along with Taylor's experiments at Bethlehem Steel in Pennsylvania, the experiments by Elton Mayo and other researchers between 1924 and 1927 at Hawthorne Works, the Western Electric plant in Cicero, Illinois, served as ground zero for positivist organizational research. Both these sets of research posited a connection between organization action and worker efficiency, assuming the predictive validity of a natural science experiment. The conclusions of these research continue to be used even in the twenty-first century by organizations such as UPS and Amazon (Robbins & Judge, 2018), testifying to the sedimented hegemony of positivism in organizational practice. Other notable proponents of positivist organizational theory included Herbert Simon, who believed that a 'pure science' approach to management was not only feasible but also often desirable (Simon, 1947). Manuals for workplace behavior often follow positivist precepts, eschewing choice in favor of replication, and measuring based on quality and efficiency.

Realism

Positivism has been criticized for its inability to deal with *unobservables*, that is, constructs that need to be theorized rather than directly tested. The development of proxies that stand in for unobservables is a hallmark of realist research (Boyd, 1991). Contrary to positivism, realism believes that observable proxies of unobservable phenomena can lead to defensible truth claims about them. Thus, it is premised on a logic of *representation*. Just as the presence of sub-atomic particles is now considered beyond doubt despite their unobservability, so too can social artifacts (e.g. culture) be considered real on the grounds of our ability to theorize them based on the observable.

Most organizational theories such as agency theory, the resource-based view of the firm, transaction cost economics, and others are predicated upon a realist perspective (Godfrey & Hill, 1995). In general, the realist perspective dominates the mainstreams of social sciences, be they sociology, economics, or political science. The task of the realist researcher is three-fold. The first is to develop proxy constructs that use observables, but represent the unobservable under study. The second is to justify the use of those constructs, through theory-building. The third task is to test and fine-tune these constructs to advance theory. For example, a researcher may use R&D expenditure as a percentage of revenues as a proxy for innovation.

The training of scholars in mainstream organizational theory is predicated upon them using methodologies and adopting an epistemological-ontological position that is consistent with realism. This has produced a rich vein of realistic theorizing in our field. Most mainstream organizational theories such as transaction costs, industry structure, and organizational boundaries that have been deployed in our field to make truth claims about management and organization emerge from a realist position (Godfrey & Hill, 1995).

Critical realism

Critical realism, which owes its popularity to the pioneering work of Roy Bhaskar (1978), has found considerable application in social sciences such as economics (Dow, 1999), sociology (Steinmetz, 1998), and organization studies (Miller & Tsang, 2011). It diverges from mainstream realism particularly in its opposition to theories such as those of Karl Popper, which offers predictive validity through statements such as 'if a, then b.' Bhaskar (1978: 69–71) argues that such laws are usually generated in 'closed systems,' where other environmental influences can be controlled, and that in the environments studied by the social sciences, such systems are neither available nor are conclusions derived from them generalizable.

Critical realists also problematize research that does not distinguish correlation from causality. They pay greater attention to the power of extrinsic and intrinsic contingencies that lead to the correlation between observed phenomena. To that end, they emphasize the role of replication in research, contending that research findings should not be generalized unless they can be replicated across samples, populations, and research methods.

To consider an example from strategy research, take the case of agency theory. One of the more influential studies in agency theory is that of Amihud and Lev (1981), which proposed that the strategic behavior of managers was greatly affected by the monitoring efforts by shareholders. This finding acquired law-like status in management theory, but was eventually contested by Lane, Cannella, and Lubatkin (1998), who used Amihud and Lev's data, augmented it with new data, and subjected it to analysis based on a slightly altered methodology, and found that Amihud and Lev's findings were not as generalizable as had been previously believed. This research may be viewed as critical realist, for it problematizes earlier laws on the grounds that they do not stand up to empirical scrutiny from multiple perspectives. The same goes for Mintzberg's (1973) reanalysis of managerial work or even stakeholder analysis, which attempts to heterogenize the concept of firm performance to include multiple perspectives.

Critical realism represents a substantial epistemological departure from mainstream realism, and that it has an important role to play in management research (Contu & Willmott, 2005). While critical realists still subscribe to the realist notion that the inherent order of things is 'mind-independent,' they place a lot more focus on the contingent relationships between phenomena and structures than mainstream realists. They are sensitive to issues of power and discourse, and the role played by dominant interests in determining what gets constituted as 'normal science.' Labor process theorists who theorize that organizational routines are ideological artifacts that aid capitalists in their attempts to extract and appropriate surplus value from the labor class may be seen as inhabiting a critical-realist paradigm (Thompson & Vincent, 2010).

Constructivism

Constructivism is guided by the assumption that the methodology of research is fundamentally theory-dependent. According to constructivists, the theoretical position held by researchers not only guides their basic position but also determines what gets construed as a research problem, what theoretical procedures are used, and what constitutes observations and evidence (Boyd, 1991: 202). Thus, constructivists challenge the notion that research is conducted by impartial, detached, value-neutral subjects, who seek to uncover clearly discernable objects or phenomena. Rather, they view researchers as craftsmen, as toolmakers (Spivey, 1995: 314) who are part of a network that creates knowledge (Law, 1992: 318) and ultimately guides practice. Ethnographers who argue that organizational identities are constructed through routines and practices can be seen as inhabiting a constructivist position.

In the field of natural sciences, we find a constructivist epistemology most clearly articulated in the work of Bruno Latour and Steve

Woolgar. In their 1979 book *Laboratory Life*, Latour and Woolgar reported on a comprehensive ethnographic analysis of a scientific laboratory at the prestigious Salk Institute for Biological Sciences in California (Latour & Woolgar, 1979/2013). They provided a granular understanding of how scientific research is conducted, the relationship between the routine work practices in the lab and the emergence of a collective understanding, the manner in which findings were deemed worthy enough to be made public, the practice of developing and publishing scientific papers, the financing of research, and other aspects of laboratory life. The book pulled the veil of the relatively opaque practice of scientific research and contributed substantially to the deepening of research sub-fields like ethnomethodology. The emergence of Actor-Network Theory as a methodology in studying the natural and social sciences can be related to this work. Constructivist epistemology developed protocols of methodological inquiry through the work of Latour and Woolgar, and subsequent works that followed it.

Pragmatism

Brief mention must be made here about philosophy of pragmatism (see Joas, 1993, for an accessible introduction). Developed in the USA in the nineteenth century by philosophers such as John Dewey and William James, pragmatism accepts that the exact relationship between positivism and constructivism is impossible to determine, but concludes therefrom that the search for such a determination is itself counterproductive. Instead, pragmatist philosophers advocate for human experience, both individual and collective, as a determining factor in courses of action. Rather than getting bogged down in theoretical matters such as induction vs. deduction, pragmatists instead favor inference, revisability, and practice. For pragmatists, the usefulness and applicability of theories are much more important than whether they are right or not, whether they define their problems elegantly or not, whether phenomena are immutable or socially constructed.

For pragmatists, words, ideas, and concepts are best thought of as inputs to a problem solving process. This would also incorporate problem solving and a move from mere description and representation of reality to acting on ones ideas to effect change. They are critical of 'philosophical fallacies,' where un-seasoned students of philosophy take conceptions such as 'the fact-value distinction' and 'the separation of the physical and mental worlds' as truths, because they do not realize that such categorizations are nothing more than mere artifacts in the minds of earlier thinkers. This attitude may be termed *anti-reification*.

The tendency to privilege epistemological thinking over empirical reasoning is a trend they seek to reverse.

Pragmatism has now found important modes of application in the field of management (see Parmar, Phillips, & Freeman, 2016: 199–211 for a comprehensive analysis). Management theorists approaching research from a pragmatist standpoint tend to develop concepts that can be researched, arguing that the best constructs are those that can be *studied*, and that the fact that they represent the concept they are designed to imperfectly is something that we must take in our stride. For example, we all know that Hambrick and Mason's idea of using demographic variables to model CEO behavior (Hambrick & Mason, 1984) is inadequate. But to the extent that this model advances research, its imperfections must be discounted. Likewise, in the field of knowledge management, theorists have argued for an explicitly pragmatic approach. Blosch (2001) critiques representations of knowledge that are excessively theoretical, inward-gazing, and non-specific. Connecting his logic to the traditions of pragmatism, he advances an approach to knowledge that could provide managers with the tools needed in order to create knowledge-based organization. Building on contemporary pragmatism, Blosch develops a definition of knowledge which would advance organizational approaches to knowledge management, and that may help managers get by in an atmosphere of rapid technological change.

The political dimension

A philosophical position is of course intertwined inescapably with the political. In their celebrated work *Sociological Paradigms and Organizational Analysis*, Gibson Burrell and Gareth Morgan represented this relationship in a Cartesian frame, with one axis representing philosophical positions divided into subjective and objective approaches to reality and the other a political frame, divided into sociologies of regulation and radical change (Burrell & Morgan, 1979). The actual mapping of theoretical positions can be framed differently, but Burrell and Morgan framework suggests that different epistemological and ontological approaches can combine with different political positions to produce *paradigms*, or spaces of shared assumptions where conversations do not have to re-articulate their assumptions fully, but can proceed with an understanding of a certain level of philosophical congruity. On the political side, those subscribing to the idea of regulation tend to idealize market-defined modes of exchange and not have as much of a problem with imbedded inequalities. Those favoring radical change tend to see the status quo as inherently unjust, and find class divisions problematic.

The political dimension to philosophy is extensively covered in Chapter 3. At this moment, it is important to say that the decision to consider or ignore the sociopolitical status quo is itself a philosophical act. By way of providing an example, we would like to discuss the intensification of inequality in US society in 2021.

As we crested the temporal milestone of 2020 and took stock of the year that was, three startling facts confronted us. The first was that the USA lost over 7% of its jobs (11 million jobs) in 2020.[1] The numbers, prosaic though they may be, conceal untold misery, of people struggling to get by, of dreams deferred, and youth squandered. The second fact was that over 400,000 deaths in 2020 could be attributed to COVID.[2] In the final three months of 2020, the USA lost more people every day due to the virus than perished in the September 11, 2001 attacks. It would be safe to say that the economic and human toll of the catastrophe was incalculable.

But perhaps it is the third fact that should give the student of organizational philosophy the greatest pause, especially in light of the first two. During the period of the pandemic, while the USA was losing jobs and lives, the US stock market was outperforming itself. During 2020, the S&P 500 went up 15%.[3] The market produced incalculable rewards for those at the top rung of the ladder. Elon Musk's net worth is now greater than the GDP of Greece, and if Jeff Bezos were a country, he would be the 50th richest in the world. It is very clear that the investing class of the world has realized to a great degree of confidence in the recent past that whatever economic pain may accrue on account of the pandemic, it can easily be pushed down to the lower rungs of the non-investing class.

The world of academia mirrors this trend. In 2020, administrator salaries in the USA rose, while colleges and universities slashed budgets, revoked tenure, refused to fill vacant positions, and brazenly repudiated existing agreements with the teaching community.[4] Faculty members 'voluntarily' submitted to furloughs and lost approved sabbaticals, and some universities issued letters of termination to their entire teaching workforce, so that they could retain the 'flexibility' to downsize at will, at a moment of their choosing. The institutional leadership invoked *force majeure* clauses, claiming the virus to be that 'act of God' which liberated them from keeping their promises.

What lies ahead for the organizational philosopher? At any point in time there are such data, ripe with political and philosophical implications, which need to be taken into account as we proceed with our understanding of concepts, constructs, and ideas.

Summing up

To reiterate, ontological, epistemological, and methodological assumptions in theory and research tend to be correlated, to that extent, a philosophical position such as positivist, realist, critical realist, constructivist, or pragmatist refer to closely banded assumptions. Positivists and realists may be visualized as holding a flashlight in a dark room. They illuminate different aspects of existing reality, while throwing others into the shadows. Enough flashlights, and the entire room becomes visible and mappable. Critical realists believe so too, except that they pay special attention to which part of the room is lit and which part is left dark, imputing agency and ideology to the research process. Constructivists on the other hand see reality as a lump of clay that the researcher then fashions into a shape, and the reader interprets. Both the researcher and the reader engage in independent acts of creation, producing constructs that derive their legitimacy through construction. For example, they would vigorously dispute the use of financial measures to model firm performance, on the grounds that there was nothing innate about it. Pragmatists on the other hand would try and resolve the debate by asking: what is the purpose of the study and does the use of financial measures to model firm performance yield any actionable results for practitioners? If so, they are worth using, despite their flaws. Those whose philosophical positions are political determined would dispute this, pointing out that to an environmental activist, financial performance is a worthless artifact, and to a labor organizer, it may even be a symbol of poor performance.

The two subsequent chapters in this book grapple with philosophical issues without setting aside the political dimension. It must be stated at the outset that our positions tend towards the approach to radical change, though readers who do not subscribe to this position will also find our approach informative and explanatory.

Philosophy and organizational theories

The field of organization studies has, over time, developed a large number of theories with which it describes, predicts, and evaluates organizational action as well as the actions of organizational actors. It is our contention that every theory and knowledge claim is infused by a variety of philosophical assumptions as well as value-laden political positions.

Some of those positions are so obvious that they are axiomatic. For instance, we can assume that a feminist scholar will be opposed to patriarchy. But what about scholars who work on women-in-management but do not necessarily identify as feminists? For example in corporate governance literature there is an inordinate amount of research examining the implications of women having sitting on corporate boards. We could map the literature on women-in-management, and locate an entire spectrum of epistemological/ontological and political positions. Likewise, it is easy to identify the political-philosophical positions of those researchers whose approaches are critical of the mainstream. It would stand to reason that while a queer theorist would be analyzing practices of performativity[5] with as objective a lens as they could, their initial position would be critical of heteronormativity. Likewise, a Marxist researcher would analyze organizational practices through the lens of historical materialism, but would begin with a position that was critical of the regimes of capitalism. A postcolonialist would start with a priori position that the shadow of colonial relations looms large over present socio-economic relations, despite the putative departure of formal colonialism from the geopolitical space. Researchers do not need to commit to starting the process of inquiry without any preconceived sociopolitical stance; indeed, we would argue that such a 'neutral' stance is nigh impossible. Rather, what scholars need to do is to make their position transparent to their readership.

A more difficult dilemma involves the explication of the epistemological and ontological positions from which researchers come. Should researchers, even before they begin their process of inquiry, declare themselves as positivists, realists, or constructivists? Do they need to make their stance clear in their work? We believe that as long as researchers make their assumptions about the nature of the field they study, their choice of methodology and their philosophical orientation will be sufficiently transparent without any need for explicit articulation.

In order to explain this issue clearly, let us consider the field of strategic management. We choose the strategy not only because it is a well-defined and influential sub-field in management theory but also because it presents several clear illustrations of the gamut of philosophical positions along the epistemological-ontological continuum, from extreme positivism to constructivism.

The sub-discipline of strategic management has a relatively recent history. It emerged in the 1970s from the field of economics, deriving advantage from the reluctance of economists to consider the firm as a legitimate unit of analysis (see Wiersema & Bowen, 2009 for an analysis). Situating their locus of study between macroeconomics and microeconomics, early strategy scholars borrowed from the field of industrial organization to argue that firm-level decisions could be generalized into taxonomies and frameworks that would help practicing managers make decisions for the firm (1984). Influential theories such as the five-force analysis of industry structure (Porter, 1980), the more inward looking resource-based view of the firm (Wernerfelt, 1984), the idea of a corporate 'core competence' that would help a firm enter multiple product markets (Prahalad & Hamel, 1990), the tools of meta-learning and dynamic capabilities (Eisenhardt & Martin, 2000), the more processual understanding of strategy as practice (Jarzabkowski, 2004), and the concept of the microfoundations of strategy (Teece, 2007) are some of the ideas that are touted, when one reflects on the mainstream milestones of the field. Newer areas include theories of organizational strategy prior to commercialization of a product (Agarwal, Moeen, & Shah, 2017) as well as platforms as alternatives to products for firm strategy (Cusumano, Gawer, & Yoffie, 2019).

The leaders in the field of strategy have attempted to achieve paradigmatic cohesion, discouraging research that does not address what they refer to as the field's defining question: why do some firms outperform others? Perhaps because of this attitude, philosophical reflections on strategy were slow to emerge. However, over time, introspection about the philosophical underpinnings of strategy research began to emerge (Godfrey & Hill, 1995) and gain traction (Mir & Watson, 2000).

Positivism in strategic management

The best example of positivist research in strategic management is game theory (Camerer, 1991). Game theorists attempt to represent (reduce?) economic activity to a series of mathematical positions, which they then conclude would not only describe firm-level action but also predict it (Saloner, 1991). The idea that positivists employ in strategic research is to take only those elements that can be measurable, and build complex constructs from simple inputs. The results of course involve models that achieve high levels of 'reliability,' but sometimes get questioned in terms of their 'validity.' In other words, the measure what they do very well, but whether their constructs track the phenomena they purport to is a question.

Calls for 'evidence-based research' in management inquiry are implicitly positivist (Kepes, Bennett, & McDaniel, 2014). More specific to strategic management, theorists prefer benchmarking to modeling, and see the value of management academics as validating the successful actions of managers rather than providing guidance for organizational action (Pfeffer & Sutton, 2006). To that extent, positivists tend to favor the status quo over change, and are more compatible with an elite-centered approach to management.

Realism in strategic management

The positivist position continues to have a lot of traction in specific areas of strategy such as logistics management, but has come under fire when it tries to describe human action within firms, especially because of its inability to analyze the unmeasurable elements of firm action (Godfrey & Hill, 1995). For example, the upper echelons theory in strategic leadership (Hambrick & Mason, 1984) contended that since ordinary researchers would have limited access to strategic leaders in an organization, they should proceed with their research by using demographic variables (age, experience, income, etc.) to build profiles of attributes such as their leadership qualities. This assertion has been accepted by the mainstreams of the field with a rather surprising level of acceptance, perhaps for self-serving reasons.

Nonetheless, the problem of unobservables in strategy research remains. A realist perspective is better set up to analyze them (e.g. dynamic capabilities or core competences). It is important to make a key differentiation between ontological and epistemological relativism. In strategy research, as in most fields, it makes obvious sense to hold on to a notion of ontological realism, one where the existence of phenomena themselves is taken for granted. For instance, one does not need to argue that people working together produce tangible things like cars and insurance policies.

Perhaps in a case of overreach, realists began to extend their premises of universality into the epistemological realm. They made a variety of assumptions that were rarely justified or even made explicit. For example, many realist theories of strategic management assumed the existence of an overt organizational identity. They viewed the organization as an entity that was naturally efficiency-oriented, committed to maximizing its potential, and governed by a single organizational reality (Zey-Ferrell, 1981). Researchers treated theories as a measure of 'the reality out there,' rather than as a product of their authors' imaginations and negotiations. For instance, a construct like 'platform strategy,' which is nothing but a name given by managers to describe a pattern in a series of firm-level decisions, has now begun to gain the status of an intrinsic concept, like a 'truth' that was 'discovered' by that manager or theorist, rather than as a mere formalization. The conceptual dimension of philosophy is extensively covered in Chapter 2.

Constructivism in strategic management

One of the problems of a realist strategy is that the points of view of certain (usually dominant) subgroups in organizations get totalized as organizational 'reality.' For example, agency theorists represent the interests of principals as organizational interests. As mentioned earlier, strategy content researchers use financial measure to model performance, thereby representing capital market stakeholders as the sole stakeholders of the firm. Thus, while realist premises have helped us illuminate the various facets of strategy research, when deployed inflexibly, they have also obfuscated many aspects of strategy by not considering the socially constructed aspects of strategy.

Constructivism in strategy, we contend, is always performed, but never discussed, perhaps because strategy scholars worry that it presents a less 'scientific' approach, hewing dangerously close to solipsism (Waribugo & Eketu, 2016). Nevertheless, there have been several instances in the field where the conclusions of researchers paint a very constructivist picture of organizations and their environments. For instance, research in crisis management suggests that crises are often created not by the external environments, but by important organizational actors who choose to define certain events as moments of crisis (Nystrom & Starbuck, 1984). Similarly, research in environmental turbulence (Cameron, Kim, & Whetten, 1987) suggests that actions of top management teams send powerful signals to organizational constituents, and may precipitate employee action that contributes to environmental turbulence. Similar kernels of constructivist epistemology can be found in the work of Doz (1996), who studied the evolution of cooperation in strategic alliances. By labeling an inter-firm agreement as 'cooperation,' organizational actors created a greater atmosphere of trust than they would have, had they labeled it a 'contract.' Yet rarely is the performativity of either organizational actors or organizational researchers acknowledged as such.

While we have chosen to discuss strategy in this brief section to illustrate how each set of theories in our field is subject to a taxonomic analysis on account of their philosophical positions, such a position can be used to analyze a variety of theories. These include discourse theory (Iedema, 2016), feminism (Benschop & Verloo, 2016), hermeneutics (Myers, 2016), institutional theory (Edwards, 2016), Marxism (Marens & Mir, 2016), postcolonial theory (Jack, 2016), poststructuralism (Linstead, 2016), practice (Sandberg & Tsoukas, 2016), pragmatism (Parmar, Phillips, & Freeman, 2016), psychoanalysis (Gabriel, 2016), queer theory (Rumens & Tyler, 2016), and structuration (Jones, 2016).

Conclusion

In this introductory essay, we have made three important claims. The first is that irrespective of whether one thinks of philosophy explicitly, each organizational researcher is a philosopher. The second is that a philosophical position is predicated on a variety of approaches relating to ontology, epistemology, methodology, ethics, and political positions. Depending on where one stands with regard to these philosophical building blocks, their orientation may be characterized as positivist, realist, critical realist, and constructivist, with pragmatist and political considerations weighing in as well. The final point is that management theories all inhabit the same spectrum of political positions that enrich them and add to their relevance the world of firms and organizations.

We hope that this chapter has provided a broad-based survey of the terrain of philosophy, especially for the relatively unfamiliar organizational theorists. In the two chapters that follow, we highlight and develop specific philosophical approaches within management theory and subject them to scrutiny.

Notes

1 www.bls.gov/news.release/empsit.toc.htm.
2 www.nytimes.com/2021/01/17/us/covid-deaths-2020.html
3 The S&P 500 went from 3257.85 on Jan 2, 2020 to 3756.07 on December 31, 2020. See www.spglobal.com/spdji/en/indices/equity/sp-500/#overview.
4 www.nytimes.com/2020/10/26/us/colleges-coronavirus-budget-cuts.html
5 There are many understandings of the term *performativity* generally and within management and organizations specifically. For an excellent ground clearing exercise on the latter see Cabantous, Gond, Harding, and Learmonth (2016). The perspective of performativity followed here draws from authors such as Butler (1993) and Callon (2007), that is, performativity as bringing into being (including constitution of the self) through statement or citation (Gond & Cabantous, 2016).

References

Acker, S. (2000). In/out/side: Positioning the researcher in feminist qualitative research. *Resources for Feminist Research*, 28(1–2), 189–210.
Agarwal, R., Moeen, M., & Shah, S. K. (2017). Athena's birth: Triggers, actors, and actions preceding industry inception. *Strategic Entrepreneurship Journal*, 11(3), 287–305.
Al-Amoudi, I. & Mahoney, J. (2016). Ontology: Philosophical discussions and implications for organizations. In R. Mir, H. Willmott & M. Greenwood

(Eds.), *Routledge companion to philosophy in organizational studies* (pp. 15–32). London: Routledge.
Amihud, Y., & Lev, B. (1981). Risk reduction as a managerial motive for conglomerate mergers. *The Bell Journal of Economics*, *12*(2), 605–617.
Banerjee, S. B. (2000). Whose land is it anyway? National interest, indigenous stakeholders, and colonial discourses: The case of the Jabiluka uranium mine. *Organization & Environment*, *13*(1), 3–38.
Barkan, I. D. (1985). Industry invites regulation: The passage of the pure food and drug act of 1906. *American Journal of Public Health*, *75*(1), 18–26.
Benschop, Y. & Verloo, M. (2016). Feminist organizational theories: Islands of treasure. In R. Mir, H. Willmott & M. Greenwood (Eds.), *Routledge companion to philosophy in organizational studies* (pp. 100–112). London: Routledge.
Bhaskar, R. (1978). On the possibility of social scientific knowledge and the limits of naturalism. *Journal for the Theory of social Behaviour*, *8*(1), 1–28.
Bierly, P. & Chakrabarti, A. (1996). Generic knowledge strategies in the US pharmaceutical industry. *Strategic Management Journal*, *17*(2), 123–135.
Blosch, M. (2001). Pragmatism and organizational knowledge management. Knowledge and Process Management, 8(1), 39–47.
Boyd, R. (1991). Observations, explanatory power, and simplicity: Toward a non-Humean account. In R. Boyd (Ed.), The philosophy of science (pp. 349–377). Cambdridge, MA: The MIT Press.
Burrell, G., & Morgan, G. (1979). *Sociological paradigms and organizational analysis*. London: Aldershot, Gower.
Butler, J. (1993). *Bodies that matter: On the discursive limits of "sex"*. New York: Routledge.
Cabantous, L., Gond, J.-P., Harding, N., & Learmonth, M. (2016). Critical essay: Reconsidering critical performativity. *Human Relations*, *69*(2), 197–213. doi:10.1177/0018726715584690.
Callon, M. (2007). What does it mean to say that economics is performative? In D. MacKenzie, F. Muniesa & L. Siu (Eds.), *Do economists make markets? On the performativity of economics* (pp. 311–357). Princeton, NJ: Princeton University Press.
Camerer, C. F. (1991). 'Does strategy research need game theory?' *Strategic Management Journal, Winter Special Issue*, *12*, pp. 137–152.
Cameron, K. Kim, M & Whetten, D. (1987). Organizational effects of decline and turbulence. *Administrative Science Quarterly*, *32*(2), 222–240.
Churchill Jr, G. A. (1979). A paradigm for developing better measures of marketing constructs. *Journal of Marketing Research*, *16*(1), 64–73.
Contu, A., & Willmott, H. (2005). You spin me round: The realist turn in organization and management studies. *Journal of Management Studies*, *42*(8), 1645–1659.
Cusumano, M. A., Gawer, A., & Yoffie, D. B. (2019). *The business of platforms: Strategy in the age of digital competition, innovation, and power*. New York: Harper Business.

26 Everyone is a philosopher

Donaldson, L. (1995). *American anti-management theories of organization: A critique of paradigm proliferation* (Vol. 25). Cambridge: Cambridge University Press.

Dow, S. C. (1999). Post Keynesianism and critical realism: What is the connection? *Journal of Post Keynesian Economics, 22*(1), 15–33.

Doz, Y. L. (1996). The evolution of cooperation in strategic alliances: Initial conditions or learning processes? *Strategic Management Journal, 17*(S1), 55–83.

Duberley, J. & Johnson, P. (2016). Methodology: Philosophical underpinnings and their implications. In R. Mir, H. Willmott & M. Greenwood (Eds.), *Routledge companion to philosophy in organizational studies* (pp. 66–83). London: Routledge.

Edwards, T. (2016). Institutional theory: Reflections on ontology. In R. Mir, H. Willmott & M. Greenwood (Eds.), *Routledge companion to philosophy in organizational studies* (pp. 125–137). London: Routledge.

Eisenhardt, K. M., & Martin, J. A. (2000). Dynamic capabilities: What are they? *Strategic Management Journal, 21*(10–11), 1105–1121.

Foucault, M. (1983). "The order of discourse." In M. J. Shapiro (Ed.), *Language and politics* (pp. 112–127). New York: New York University Press.

Gabriel, Y. (2016). Psychoanalysis and the study of organizations. In R. Mir, H. Willmott & M. Greenwood (Eds.), *Routledge companion to philosophy in organizational studies* (pp. 212–224). London: Routledge

Ghoshal, S. (2005). Bad management theories are destroying good management practices. *Academy of Management Learning & Education, 4*(1), 75–91.

Ghoshal, S., & Moran, P. (1996). Bad for practice: A critique of the transaction cost theory. *Academy of Management Review, 21*(1), 13–47.

Godfrey, P. C., & Hill, C. W. (1995). The problem of unobservables in strategic management research. *Strategic Management Journal, 16*(7), 519–533.

Gond, J.-P., & Cabantous, L. (2016). Performativity: Towards a performative turn in organizational studies. In R. Mir, H. Willmott & M. Greenwood (Eds.), *The Routledge companion to philosophy in organization studies* (pp. 508–516). London: Routledge.

Gramsci, A., Q. Hoare, Q., & Nowell-Smith, G. (1971). *Selections from the prison notebooks of Antonio Gramsci*. London: Lawrence and Wishart.

Greenwood, M. (2016). Approving or improving research ethics in management journals. *Journal of Business Ethics, 137*(3), 507–520.

Hambrick, D. C., & Mason, P. A. (1984). Upper echelons: The organization as a reflection of its top managers. *Academy of Management Review, 9*(2), 193–206.

Iedema, R. (2016). Discourse as organizational and practical philosophy. In R. Mir, H.Willmott & M. Greenwood (Eds.), *Routledge companion to philosophy in organizational studies* (pp. 87–99). London: Routledge.

Jack, G. (2016). Postcolonial theory: Speaking back to empire. In R. Mir, H. Willmott & M. Greenwood (Eds.), *Routledge companion to philosophy in organizational studies* (pp. 151–170). London: Routledge.

Jarzabkowski, P. (2004). Strategy as practice: Recursiveness, adaptation, and practices-in-use. *Organization Studies, 25*(4), 529–560.

Jepperson, R. L. (1991), 'Institutions, institutional effects, and institutionalism.' In W. W. Powell & P. J. DiMaggio (Eds.), *The new institutionalism in organizational analysis* (pp. 143–163). Chicago: The University of Chicago Press.

Joas, H. (1993). *Pragmatism and social theory.* Chicago: University of Chicago Press.

Jones, M. (2016). Structuration theory: Philosophical stance and significance for organizational research. In R. Mir, H. Willmott & M. Greenwood (Eds.), *Routledge companion to philosophy in organizational studies* (pp. 1–17). London: Routledge.

Kaufman, A., Zacharias, L., & Karson, M. J. (1995). *Managers vs. owners: The struggle for corporate control in American democracy.* New York: Oxford University Press, USA.

Kepes, S., Bennett, A. A., & McDaniel, M. A. (2014). Evidence-based management and the trustworthiness of our cumulative scientific knowledge: Implications for teaching, research, and practice. *Academy of Management Learning & Education, 13*(3), 446–466.

Kuhn, T. S. (1970). *The structure of scientific revolutions (2nd edition).* Chicago: University of Chicago Press.

Lane, P. J., Cannella Jr, A. A., & Lubatkin, M. H. (1998). Agency problems as antecedents to unrelated mergers and diversification: Amihud and Lev reconsidered. *Strategic Management Journal, 19*(6), 555–578.

Latour, B., & Woolgar, S. (1979/2013). *Laboratory life: The construction of scientific facts.* Princeton, NJ: Princeton University Press.

Law, J. (1992). Notes on the theory of the actor-network: Ordering, strategy, and heterogeneity. *Systems Practice, 5*(4), 379–393.

Leplin, J. (1984). *Scientific realism.* Berkeley, CA: University of California Press.

Linstead, S. (2016). Poststructuralist theory: Thinking organization otherwise. In R. Mir, H. Willmott & M. Greenwood (Eds.), *Routledge companion to philosophy in organizational studies* (pp. 171–183). London: Routledge.

Marens, R. (2010). Destroying the village to save it: Corporate social responsibility, labour relations, and the rise and fall of American hegemony. *Organization, 17*(6), 743–766.

Marens, R. & Mir, R. (2016). Marxism: A philosophical analysis of class conflict. In R. Mir, H. Willmott & M. Greenwood (Eds.), *Routledge companion to philosophy in organizational studies* (pp. 138–150). London: Routledge.

Meyer, J. W. and Rowan, B. (1991), Institutionalized organizations: Formal structure as myth and ceremony. In W. W. Powell & P. J. DiMaggio (Eds.), *The new institutionalism in organizational analysis* (pp. 41–62). Chicago: The University of Chicago Press.

Miller, K. D., & Tsang, E. W. (2011). Testing management theories: Critical realist philosophy and research methods. *Strategic Management Journal, 32*(2), 139–158.

Mintzberg, H. (1973). *The nature of managerial work*. London: Harper & Row.
Mir, R. (2018). Embracing qualitative research: An act of strategic essentialism. *Qualitative Research in Organizations and Management*, *13*(4), 306–314.
Mir R. & Watson, A. (2000). Strategic management and the philosophy of science: Imperatives for a constructivist methodology, *Strategic Management Journal*, *21*(9), 1–13.
Mir R. & Watson, A. (2001). Critical realism and constructivism in strategy research: Toward a synthesis, *Strategic Management Journal*, *22*(12), 101–105.
Mir, R. Willmott, H. & Greenwood, M. (2016). *Routledge companion to philosophy in organizational studies*. London: Routledge.
Morgan, G., & Smircich, L. (1980). The case for qualitative research. *Academy of Management Review*, *5*(4), 491–500.
Myers, M. (2016). Hermeneutics in organization studies. In R. Mir, H. Willmott & M. Greenwood (Eds.) *Routledge companion to philosophy in organizational studies* (pp. 113–124). London: Routledge.
Nystrom, P. C., & Starbuck, W. H. (1984). To avoid organizational crises, unlearn. *Organizational Dynamics*, *12*(4), 53–65.
O'Connor, M. (1989). Codependency and indeterminacy: A critique of the theory of production. *Capitalism Nature Socialism*, *1*(3), 33–57.
Parmar, B. Phillips, R. & Freeman, RE. (2016). Pragmatism and organization studies. In R. Mir, H. Willmott & M. Greenwood (Eds.), *Routledge companion to philosophy in organizational studies* (pp. 199–211). London: Routledge.
Perrow, C. (1994). Pfeffer slips! *Academy of Management Review*, *19*(2), 191–194.
Pfeffer, J. (1993). Barriers to the advance of organizational science: Paradigm development as a dependent variable. *Academy of Management Review*, *18*(4), 599–620.
Pfeffer, J., & Sutton, R. I. (2006). Evidence-based management. *Harvard Business Review*, 84(1), 62–68.
Porter, M. E. (1980). *Competitive strategy: Measuring business excellence*. New York: The Free Press.
Prahalad, C. K., & Hamel, G. (1990). The core competence of the corporation. International Library of Critical Writings in Economics, 163, 210–222.
Prasad, P. (1997). 'Systems of meaning: Ethnography as a methodology for the study of information technologies.' In A. Lee & J. Degross (Eds.), *Qualitative methods and information research* (pp. 1–30). Kluwer Academic Press, Boston, MA.
Rishi, M., & Singh, A. (2011). Corporate governance and international best practices: The case of Satyam. *Journal of Services Research*, *11*(1), 121–132.
Robbins, S. P., & Judge, T. A. (2018). *Organizational behavior* (18th edition). New Jersey: Prentice Hall.
Rowlinson, M., & Hassard, J. (1994). Economics, politics, and labour process theory. *Capital & Class*, *18*(2), 65–97.

Rumens, N. & Tyler, M. (2016). Queer theory. In R. Mir, H. Willmott & M. Greenwood (Eds.), *Routledge companion to philosophy in organizational studies* (pp. 225–236). London: Routledge.

Saloner, G. (1991). 'Modeling, game theory, and strategic management', *Strategic Management Journal, Winter Special Issue*, 12, 119–136.

Sandberg, J. & Tsoukas, H. (2016). Practice theory: What it is, what it does, and what it offers organization studies: Life, knowledge and disruption. In R. Mir, H. Willmott & M. Greenwood (Eds.), *Routledge companion to philosophy in organizational studies* (pp. 184–198). London: Routledge.

Scherer, A. Does, E. & Marti, E. (2016). Epistemology: Philosophical foundations and organizational controversies. In R. Mir, H. Willmott & M. Greenwood (Eds.), *Routledge companion to philosophy in organizational studies* (pp. 33–50). London: Routledge.

Schlick, M. (1991). Positivism and realism. In R. Boyd, P. Gaspar & J. Trout (Eds.), *The philosophy of science* (pp. 37–55). Cambridge, MA: The MIT Press.

Simon, H. A. (1947). A comment on "the science of public administration". *Public Administration Review*, 7(3), 200–203.

Spivey, N. N. (1995). *Written discourse: A constructivist perspective*. In L. P. Steffe & J. E. Gale (Eds.), *Constructivism in education* (pp. 313–329). Mahwah, NJ: Lawrence Erlbaum Associates, Inc.

Steinmetz, G. (1998). Critical realism and historical sociology. A review article. *Comparative Studies in Society and History*, 40(1), 170–186.

Sutton, R. I., & Staw, B. M. (1995). What theory is not. *Administrative Science Quarterly*, 40(3), 371–384.

Taylor, F. W. (1911). *The principles of scientific management*. New York: Harper & Brothers.

Teece, D. J. (2007). Explicating dynamic capabilities: The nature and microfoundations of (sustainable) enterprise performance. *Strategic Management Journal*, 28(13), 1319–1350.

Thompson, P., & Vincent, S. (2010). Labour process theory and critical realism. In P. Thompson & C. Smith (Eds.), *Working life: Renewing labour process analysis* (pp. 47–69). Houndmills, UK: Palgrave Macmillan.

Uebel, T. E. (Ed.). (2012). *Rediscovering the forgotten Vienna circle: Austrian studies on Otto Neurath and the Vienna circle* (Vol. 133). Vienna: Springer Science & Business Media.

Von Glaserfeld, E. (1995). A constructivist approach to teaching. In L. Steffe & J. Gale (Eds.), *Constructivism in education* (pp. 113–128). Hillsdale, NJ: Lawrence Erlbaum.

Waribugo, S., & Eketu, D. (2016). Solipsism in social inquiry: Revisiting a redundant paradigm. *International Journal of Advanced Academic Research: Social and Management Sciences*, 2(4), 18–25.

Weick, K. E. (1995). What theory is not, theorizing is. *Administrative Science Quarterly*, 40(3), 385–390.

Wernerfelt, B. (1984). A resource-based view of the firm. *Strategic Management Journal*, 5(2), 171–180.

Wiersema, M. F., & Bowen, H. P. (2009). The use of limited dependent variable techniques in strategy research: Issues and methods. *Strategic Management Journal, 30*(6), 679–692.

Williamson, O. (1985). *The economic institutions of capitalism: Firms, markets, relational contracting*. NY: The Free Press.

Williamson, O. E. (1996). Economic organization: The case for candor. *Academy of Management Review, 21*(1), 48–57.

Wray-Bliss, E. (2016). Ethical philosophy, organization studies and good suspicion. In R. Mir, H. Willmott & M. Greenwood (Eds.), *Routledge companion to philosophy in organizational studies* (pp. 51–65). London: Routledge.

Zey-Ferrell, M. (1981). Criticisms of the dominant perspective on organizations. *The Sociological Quarterly, 22*(2), 181–205.

Zyphur, M. J., & Pierides, D. C. (2020). Statistics and probability have always been value-laden: An historical ontology of quantitative research methods. *Journal of Business Ethics, 167*(1), 1–18.

2 Interrogating concepts

Introduction

Concepts are foundational both to philosophy and to management studies. Yet the understanding of concepts – what they are, how they come to be, and what purposes they serve – differs widely across these fields. This chapter will examine these questions, consider how concepts have been used in management studies, and proffer a deeper use of concepts as method for management research. The underlying theses of the chapter are that concepts are fundamental to how we know the world and that concepts can provide a bridge between philosophy and management studies.

In management theory we use concepts ostensibly in order to understand, explain, predict, and (occasionally) problematize management and organizations. Consider the area of strategic management as an example; we use prosaic concepts like 'SWOT analysis' and the 'five forces' to explain the strategic behavior of organizations, but we also employ more abstract and multifaceted concepts like 'performance' and 'effectiveness' as key underpinnings to such analyses. Concepts drive and constitute what we count as our knowledge. Across ontological positions it may be claimed that "we cannot gain access to the world independently of the concepts we use" (Fleetwood & Ackroyd, 2005: 3) Yet, even in the most highly regarded scholarship that engages deeply with concepts, often scant attention is paid to their conception and how they are conceived, and probably even less attention is paid to their performativity (Greenwood & Van Buren, 2017). If philosophy is the practice of the creation of concepts (Deleuze & Guattari, 1994) and the proper role for research is the production of ideas (Lyotard, 1984), then philosophy is the perfect schema from which to interrogate the use of concepts in management research.

DOI: 10.4324/9781351030700-2

Hence, this chapter will unfold in three parts: (1) it will explore the concept of concept, the link between concepts and philosophy, and the related link between philosophy and social science; (2) it will look at how concepts have been used in management and organization studies; and (3) it will reimagine concepts as methods *qua* provocation to some of our methodological practices. The aim of the chapter is to restore concepts to their rightful significance in the development of management knowledge.

Concepts as creative and reductive: addressing the nature and purposes of concepts

Concepts are fundamental to the very essence of philosophy, yet are also core to the inquiry of social science. Concepts are derivative from past knowledge, but are also creative of new knowledge. Concepts by their very nature rely on abstraction and ambivalence, however are undone by those very processes. Not all concepts are created equal; some are more conceptual than others. Concepts, we will argue, provide an invaluable connection between philosophical questions and social science methods, a problem patent in management and organization studies.

Concepts are not ready-made hermetically sealed devices available to be seamlessly transported and plugged into a theory or a model. They do not arrive without history, without genre, and without organization. Yet, they are made and remade in their very use. They are constructed and validated in the context of who is speaking, from what institutional site, and from what subject position (Foucault, 1972). This paradoxical nature of concepts, as being both old and new, as having both an origin and needing to be created, is explored here in order to explicate what makes a concept a concept, what work concepts do, and how concepts are organized and organize.

Concepts in philosophy and social science

By responding to the question "what is philosophy?" with the answer that "philosophy is the art of forming, inventing, and fabricating concepts," Deleuze and Guattari (1994) leave us in no doubt that philosophy is nothing without concepts and that concepts are nothing if not philosophical. Deleuze and Guattari (1994) speak of a 'small p' philosophy, one that rails against the 'big P' philosophy of meta-theorizing, grand narratives, and the search for ultimates, in which "the concern for enforcing rules limits utility for solving problems" (Jackson & Carter,

2007: 147). In contrast, philosophy is a creative process, the sole purpose of which is to contribute to the solution of problems. Philosophy should invent new ways of thinking and, hence, the role of the concept is to "intervene ontologically in the world, and *through this intervention* create something interesting, remarkable, or important" (Kristensen, Lopdrup-Hjorth, & Sørensen, 2014: 499). "Philosophy then becomes the dual act of disruption and creation, leading us back to life itself" (Mir, Willmott, & Greenwood, 2016: 6).

Concepts should never be considered "ready-made," rather they must be constructed afresh in ever use and be specific to every field (Deleuze & Guattari, 1994). In the words of Deleuze and Guattari (1994: 7), "every creation is singular, and the concept as a specifically philosophical creation is always a singularity." We should be deeply distrustful of all concepts taken from elsewhere. This position follows from Nietzsche (1968: 220, §409) when he wrote that philosophers "must no longer accept concepts as a gift, nor merely purify and polish them, but first make and create them, present them and make them convincing."

Whereas philosophers may see concepts as creative, social science has traditionally seen concepts as derivative from our experience of the world. Alfred Schutz (1972/1953) articulated an understanding of concepts as second order constructs, an idea that seems to have been both forgotten and appropriated by management studies. As early as 1953, Schutz (1972/1953: 62–63) claims concepts as subjective abstraction or interpretation from other actors' sense-making:

> The basic insight that the concepts formed by the social scientist are constructs of the constructs formed in common-sense thinking by the actors on the social scene offers an answer [to the vexed question of] How is it possible to form objective concepts and an objectively verifiable theory of subjective meaning-structures?

Hence, we can differentiate between a primary or literal signifier, a first order technical denoted meaning, and a secondary signified meaning of meaning, in which the symbolic or sacred resides, a figurative meaning that is bound to the literal meaning, and vice versa. According to Paul Ricoeur (1970: 29), the "scientist" can and must practice within the limits of a neutral attitude of description by "bracketing absolute reality and of every question related to the absolute." In contrast, for the philosopher, the object must be 'sacred' because, in the words of Ricoeur (1970: 29), "why would I be interested in [considering] the object… if I did not expect from within this understanding, this something to 'address' itself to me?" Ricoeur's contrast between science and philosophy beggars the question of how to locate where to conceive management studies.

Management studies has generally followed social science in its understanding of concepts, more or less emphasizing their derivation from observed social phenomenon and bracketing questions of absolute validity. Early in the development of the field, in the influential journal *Academy of Management Review*, concepts were defined "as a broad mental configuration of a given phenomenon" (Bacharach, 1989: 500) and as "meaning-laden classifications that serve as building blocks of science" (Osigweh, 1989: 591) acknowledging that, although they purportedly derive from observation, concepts are imbued with cognitive frames and meaning. However, despite demanding clarity of others in the use of concepts in management studies (e.g., Suddaby, 2010), those who debate the concept of concept are often imprecise, even using the term concept as a synonym for or interchangeably with the term construct (e.g., Bacharach, 1989; Bort & Kieser, 2011).

At a minimum, using the devices of these very management scholars and without recourse to philosophical thinking, concepts can be readily differentiated from constructs. If variables are 'observed units' and constructs are 'approximated units' (Bacharach, 1989: 498) then, we extrapolate, concepts can be understood as abstract or 'abstracted units.' Put differently, and returning to Schutz (1953), concepts are the construct of constructs. If concepts are the building blocks of theory, then they need to be working at a higher level than that attributed to constructs (i.e. a categorization of the empirical world). This then leaves management studies with the problem of abstraction and the desire to create ideas afresh, a much worthier concern than the banal preoccupation with construct redundancy (see Banks, Gooty, Ross, Williams, & Harrington, 2018).

In sum, both philosophy and social science might understand concepts as a form of abstraction; however, they are likely to disagree about from what this higher form has been abstracted. These understandings are depicted in Table 2.1, alongside our proposal regarding the depiction of concepts in management studies. We posit that management studies, if it were to be explicit and clear, would interpret concepts as abstracted units that form the core of a theoretical schema selected to explore observed units, and that are operationalized for purposes of this exploration through proxy or approximated units known as constructs (as noted) in Table 2.1.

Concepts as abstraction and classification

From its conception, the word concept displays the seemingly contradicting ideas of 'creating in the mind' and 'taking from the world.'

Table 2.1 Understandings of concepts

Levels of abstraction		Philosophy (creating concepts)	Philosophy (interpreting concepts)	Social science	Management studies
Lower	1.	Images, thoughts, etc., that "arise in the spirit"	Noetic intention = literal meaning	Data	Observed units
	2.	Words = similar images for which one word exists	Noematic intention = sacred meaning	First order constructs	Construct = approximated units
Higher	3.	Concepts = a collection of images with some words nonvisible but audible	Concepts = meaning of meaning	Concepts = second order constructs	Concepts = abstracted units
		Nietzsche (1968/1901)	Ricoeur (1970)	Schutz (1972/1953)	Adapted from Bacharach[1] (1989)

Consider its etymology *con* (know) + *capere* (take) and these definitions selected from the Oxford Dictionary (Friedrichsen & Onions, 1973: 388–389):

> **Concept** An idea of a class of objects, general notion 1663. Concepts are merely the results, rendered permanent by language, or a previous process of comparison SIR W. HAMILITON
>
> **Conception** The action or faculty of forming a concept. That which is conceived in the mind; an idea, notion 1526.

Concepts live and die through abstraction; it is through abstraction that concepts tell both the truth and the lies. Nietzsche (1954/1873), taking a broad view of concepts, tells us that every word is a concept as it is a signifier of a larger category, which is, in turn, a reminder of an infinite number of more or less similar cases. Similarly, Zygmunt Bauman (1991) suggests that the very act of naming, that is the function of language, is an act of classification and ordering. If I say I am sitting at my table, you do not need to know of the exact table or precisely my posture in order to understand or imagine me. When using words as representation for the purposes of description or communication, we abstract from unique individual instances to a generic denotation of the same class. Hence, according to Nietzsche (1968/1901: 46), "every concept originates through our equating what is unequal" and, as such, every abstraction is a truth but also a lie.

Classification is fundamental not only to how we know the world, as previously noted, but also to how we control and shape it:

> To classify, in other words, is to give the world a *structure:* to manipulate its probabilities; to make some events more likely than some others; to behave as if events were not random, or to limit or eliminate randomness of events.
>
> (Bauman, 1991: 1, his emphasis)

Yet inherent to classification is ambivalence, the "possibility of assigning an object or event to more than one category," which causes anxiety and indecision, a threat to order and control (Bauman, 1991: 1). Indeed, it is precisely this moment of disruption or undecidability that opens possibilities for acts of creativity and moral responsibility (Clegg, Kornberger, & Rhodes, 2007). Concepts can be used to group and name; characteristics and behaviors can be attributed; criteria for inclusion/exclusion developed; constructs extracted, measured, and reported. In this way we can know and direct an orderly world. However, concepts can also create, can fill a void, can imagine something new, can name something previously absent or there but not visible, can disorder the world. According to Deleuze and Guattari (1994), a concept is composed of distinct but inseparable components; it is always greater than the sum of its parts, and therefore always doing something new.

Whether an act of classification or an act of creation, concepts are second order or meta-discourses (i.e. constructs of constructs or meanings of meanings as shown in Table 2.1) and, therefore, performative at several levels. Michel Foucault (1972: 49) proffered that we face "(a) task that consists of not – of no longer – treating discourses as groups of signs (signifying elements referring to contents or representations) but as practices that systematically form the objects of which they speak." According to Nietzsche (1968/1901), our drive to form concepts is not to understand the world but rather to organize it.

Concepts as thick and thin

Thus far concepts have been described as philosophical and scientific, as acts of creation and acts of derivation, and as tools for abstraction and tools for classification and control. Concepts have also be described as varying, for want of a better word, in quality: as extensive or intensive (Colebrook, 2017) and as thick or thin (Väyrynen, 2017). Extensive concepts are generic ideas that can be defined by their use as a label or category (e.g. the term 'research' might be a label applied to that which is published in a refereed journal or that which falls under the categories required by university metrics). In contrast, intensive concepts do something new; they think beyond the actual, and they require us to think or act differently (e.g. the term 'research' may be used to reframe seemingly unrelated data as a body of knowledge or reframe a particular communication as inquiry). Concepts can also be described as thick or thin – drawn from the notion of thin and thick description – based on criteria related to both type and degree (Väyrynen, 2017). Thin concepts tend[2] to be either descriptive (e.g. length) or evaluative (e.g. bad) in nature, whereas thick concepts are both descriptive and evaluative (e.g. kindness). Thin concepts tend to oversimplify and generalize, whereas thick concepts are more situationally specific and multifaceted.

Despite not generalizing in an empirical sense, intensive concepts by virtue of their newness have a capacity to shock and stick and, as such are more likely to be useful and meaningful; they can provoke new ways of thinking that could inform our understanding of other contexts (i.e. have conceptual generalizability; see Green & Thorogood, 2018). However, extensive concepts, by virtue of their applicability and adaptability across a range of interests, are more likely to be broadly disseminated and embraced (i.e. have interpretative viability; see Benders & Van Veen, 2001). For example, early in its development, the conceptual breadth of stakeholder theory was noted as one of its "greatest strengths [but] also one of its most prominent theoretical liabilities as a topic of reasoned discourse" (Phillips, Freeman, & Wicks, 2003: 479). This opens the idea that thick concepts can and should be both intensive and extensive.

In this chapter we will use the term *thick concept* to refer to a concept that is both extensive and intensive and that both describes and evaluates, and the term *thin concept* to refer to its inferior counterpart. We refer to the process of weakening a concept, that is destroying its intensity and thickness, as *thinning,* a topic to which we will return. Hence, a thick concept is one that is both richly descriptive and evaluative (thick), creates something new in its deep situatedness (intensive), and has conceptual generalizability (extensive). However it is important, and in keeping with the spirit of the thick use of concepts, that we explicate that our conceptualization of concepts is founded on three presumptions regarding these descriptors: that they are not binary or exclusive categories but rather heuristics; that they are not fixed, essential characteristics but rather potentialities; and that they are not morally neutral but rather more or less ethical. Thus the notion of thick or thin concepts is more precisely understood as thick or thin *use of* concepts, whereby the thin use of concepts or the thinning of concepts might be deemed to be abuse.

The politics of thickening and thinning of concepts

The thickening of concepts, akin to the search for meaning in text, must be undertaken through a restoration of meaning based on a critical trust (i.e. what Ricoeur (1970) referred to as a hermeneutics of faith) and through a demystification of illusion and an opposition to the sacred (i.e. a hermeneutics of suspicion, ibid.). Nietzsche (1968/1901: 221) cautioned against the trusting of concepts and claimed "what is needed above all is an absolute skepticism toward all inherited concepts." Ricoeur (1970: 33) is at pains to note that the destruction embedded in such suspicion is in fact "beyond destruction" and "is a moment of every new foundation." Our doubts and puzzlements bring about states of impasse or *apoira* that can be starting points (Jones & ten Bos, 2007; Mir *et al.*, 2016). Indeed, wonder seems an appropriate response to an object that surprises us, and organization can be both glorious and grotesque, and which invokes all kinds of affects (Jones & ten Bos, 2007). Hence, "if we claim that organizations should be a philosophical subject, then it is because organization makes us anxious, curious, angry, hopeful doubtful and confused" (ibid.: 3).

In contrast, a thinning of concepts is undertaken through faith without suspicion or suspicion without faith. In absence of belief in or care for the object, meaning is not enhanced but reduced. This reduction can occur by demarcating concepts in terms of their causes (e.g. psychological or social antecedents), their function (e.g. affective, ideological, technical), or their genesis (e.g. individual, historical) (Ricoeur, 1970: 28). For instance, a critical reading of the traditional histories of concepts would have us understanding these histories as 'legitimating' what is already known and closing down of alternatives (Cummings, Bridgman, Hassard, & Rowlinson, 2017; Foucault, 1990: 9). The history of concepts is not the "stone-by-stone construction of an edifice," but rather "a field of statements where they appeared and circulated" (Foucault, 1972: 56). Foucault is concerned with these statements' anonymous dispersion through texts, books, and oeuvres and the "procedures of intervention" that may be legitimately applied to concepts. The procedures that may be used include *rewriting* in a different form (e.g. from narrative to tables), *transcribing* in different language (e.g. from natural language to jargon), *translating* quantitative statements into qualitative formulations and vice versa, *approximation* to increase refine their exactitude, *delimitation* that extends or restricts the domain of validity, *transfer* of a type of statement from one field to another, *systematizing* by linking statements or redistributing statements that have previously been linked. Such interventions, some formal and some rhetorical, act on texts internally and externally (i.e. between) and are practices that (re)produce and disperse concepts, "and constitute partial organizations among themselves" (Foucault, 1972: 60).

Concepts as commodities: addressing the thinning of concepts in management studies

From the vantage point of the last decade of the millennium, Deleuze and Guattari (1994) were deeply concerned about the commodification of concepts. In their reading, philosophy has moved through three phases in relation to the use of concepts: a first age as an *encyclopedia* of concepts, the cataloguing and perfecting of universal abstract concepts; a second age as a *pedagogy* of concepts, the training in the practice of concepts, how concepts are formed, organized, and legitimized in situ; and a third age of the concept, that of *commercial professional training,* in which concepts are commodified by 'experts' and traded in markets. Forecasted as part of the post-modern condition, the production and legitimation of knowledge that is driven by technical claims[3] (understood as efficiency in achieving performance goals) have perverted the role of research; indeed, it "terrorises the production of ideas" (Lyotard, 1984; Woodard, 2018, n.p.). Management scholars become but one example of the "calamitous and insolent ... ideas men" in a race for a "marketable form of the concept" (Deleuze & Guattari, 1994: 10–11).

Concepts as fashion in management studies

Concepts rise and fall in management and organization studies. Indeed, "organizational science is characterized by its attention to successive concepts" (Hirsch & Levin, 1999: 199) to the point that concepts are often labeled as fashion and fads and dismissed as being the chattels of management consultants and gurus; consider any number of past examples available in airport bookstands from TQM to emotional intelligence. Initial discussion regarding shifts in concept popularity was framed in terms of the diffusion and rejection of innovations in management thinking, and explained using institutional theory that assumed on the rational actors bounded by formal systems (Abrahamson, 1991; Abrahamson & Fairchild, 1999). Only slight reference was made in this early work to the political or symbolic elements of concept use: the political contexts in which concepts are constructed; the political activities in academic publishing, for example when authors "use the term loosely to tie their work to a conceptually rising star" but later might find themselves challenged by reviewers to carefully define their use (Hirsh & Levin, 1999: 206); or the symbolic use of concepts in management practice to show alignment with industry leaders, signal certain characteristics, or to build legitimacy (Abrahamson, 1999).

Using the *language of biology*, which was itself a fashion of the time, authors employed "an ecological theory of fashions and institutions" (Hirsch & Levin, 1999: 9) and "a life-cycle model" to suggest that there are progressive, even naturally occurring, temporal elements to concept adoption and disbandment. According to Hirsch and Levin (ibid.: 199), concepts or what they term 'umbrella constructs' come to life at the behest of big picture proponents or 'umbrella advocates' based on their initial face validity, and then are put to death based on a lack of construct validity at the judgment of 'validity police' in a world of post-positivist organizational science. Yet even at this early stage of the debate, there were hints that concepts may infiltrate management and organization studies in ways other than through empirical hypo-deductive methods, and that there is a political dimension to knowledge production.

Empirical investigation of how management scholars use concepts has employed the *language of markets*, similarly a fashion of particular times. Bort and Shiller-Merkins (2011) trace over several decades how many and which kinds of concepts have been successful in the field of organizational studies and conclude that concepts that allow scholars to (1) balance a demand for both novelty and continuity and (2) align with dominant logic of positivism are popular because they reduce uncertainty within research and publishing institutions. Bort and Kieser (2011) investigate "the market for scholarly publishing" and found that the use of concepts varied with the reputation of the authors of the concept, the outlets in which it was published, and the provision of a method for empirical analysis. They conclude that "fashion is prevalent in organization theory"[4] (Bort & Kieser, 2011: 672) where the concept of fashion, never elucidated by the authors, seems to be a underspecified stand-in for that which drives research other than "the search for truth alone" (ibid.: 655).

As an amusing and not irrelevant aside, John Elkington (2018) announced in the ultimate business 'fashion' magazine, *Harvard Business Review*, what he calls the first ever voluntary "management concept recall." The reasons for Elkington's recall of the triple bottom line (also known as TBL and 3BL) on its 25th anniversary are not entirely clear, but seem to include: that the concept has been adopted by business but it has not changed the fundamental core of capitalism; that there are some companies that have changed for the better but others that have not; and that we need a "new wave of TBL" and he has a consultancy company ready to assist. Elkington's (2018, n.p.) salient point is that management concepts "operate in poorly regulated environments where failures are often brushed under boardroom or faculty carpets" yet "can jeopardize lives in the air, at sea, on roads or in hospitals [and] can also put entire businesses and sectors at risk." Management concepts, such as TBL, can have profound effect on the shaping knowledge and practice in organizations and the lives of many, sometimes involuntary and unaware, stakeholders (e.g. which workers in Bangladeshi clothing factories have consented to Puma's 'Environmental Profit & Loss approach' that is lauded by Elkington).

Hence, the discussion on fads in management studies raises questions, such as those posed by Bort and Kieser (2011), as to whether fashion is negative or positive, whether it is unavoidable, and whether it is affected by institutional technologies (e.g. journal ranking). The answer is yes to all of the above and more. Academic knowledge is driven by "fashion" and "concepts are carriers of fashion" (ibid.: 656). And this can drive scholars to produce regurgitated, incremental, generalizing, gap-spotting 'chaff' (Starbuck, 2009) if this seems to be the safe bet at the time. However, the very same scholars can dedicate themselves to 'problematization' (Alvesson & Sandberg, 2011), a concept which is having its day, just as soon as the right scholar in the right journal tells them that they should. Thus, the concept of problematization, which has "taken the western world by storm" (Bacchi, 2015: 1), should itself be problematized. Following a Foucauldian emphasis on how issues have been problematized and how knowledge constitutes subjects, it could be suggested that the concept of problematization has been used to (re)present knowledge or the knower as having critical intent (Bacchi, 2015) or being with the zeitgeist. Concepts are not merely carriers of knowledge; they are carriers of and constitute knowledge, ideologies, subjects, and subject positions.

We take these seeds of thoughts forward by examining two instances of concept use in management studies and by considering some general issues of ethics and politics in the concept use.

Two examples of concept use in management studies

Justice for justice

In pursuit of justice for justice, Rhodes (2016) provides an incisive analysis of how one of the oldest concepts in Western philosophy has been uprooted from its origins and transcribed and transferred (see Foucault, 1990) into social science as *organizational justice*. From an Aristotelian lens, justice is a virtue that is distinguished from other virtues as being concerned, not only with individual character and capacity but also with the condition of other persons and fairness and equality within communities. In management studies, the ancient distinction of justice as fairness has been reduced to two concepts, the concept of distributive justice (fairness of outcomes) and procedural justice (fairness of process that lead to outcomes). However, a third concept was later included, that of interpersonal justice (fairness of interpersonal treatment and provision of information) (Bies, 2005). Despite recognition that organizational justice is necessarily understood in terms of the perception of those at the receiving end, the concept has been developed as purportedly value-free, and as such measurable and manipulatable. This treatment of justice as a variable is based on 'crude bifurcation' (Rhodes 2016: 451), which suggests that while philosophers might be concerned with providing prescriptive or normative accounts of justice, social scientists need to merely describe and analyze individual's perceptual cognition of justice. This allowing for two salutary observations.

First, that the thinning of the concept of justice is premised on the spurious distinction between facts and values. As noted by Ricoeur (1970: 21–22) any word, indeed "voiced sound endowed with significance," can be understood as an act of interpretation (i.e. "to say something of something") and therefore ripe with contextually embedded meanings and values. In the world as we experience it, facts and values cannot be fully separated (Putnam, 2002). Rather, most facts are institutionally embedded and, as such, presuppose values constitutive of those institutions (Searle, 1964). Furthermore, given that our institutions are constituted by statements that involve obligations, commitments, and responsibilities, concepts such as justice have enormous capacity to form and perform structures and actions that affect our very existence (Greenwood & Van Buren, 2017).

Second, and relatedly, the organizational justice, formed as it is a descriptive social science concept, is presented as agnostic as the service to which it is put. It is hard to imagine the scientist who, according to Ricoeur (1970: 29), unlike the philosopher who cannot avoid the question of absolute validity of the object, "can and must practice this method of bracketing ... of absolute reality and or every question concerning the absolute." Another version of the crude bifurcation would have us believe that social science is non-prescriptive. Yet, every study has a purpose (or multiple purposes if you count the scholar's goal of achieving tenure) and many studies invoking this concept take as their goal, explicitly or implicitly, proof that organizational justice enhances organization performance (Fortin & Fellenz, 2008).

Whose culture is it anyway?

In what could be described as a value-loss chain, the concept of culture has traveled from anthropological studies through to Geert Hofstede,[5] through to management scholarly and practitioner derivatives of Hofstede, on to derivatives of these derivatives, and into the tool kit for interculturist consultants. In short, this rich, deep concept has been imported into management studies and practice only to be thinned and commodified.

In *Culture's Consequences*, Hofstede (1980: 4) provides his definition of culture as "collective programming of the mind" and explicitly identifies this as resembling Pierre Bourdieu's concept of habitus. He presents a figure in the form of a triangle that depicts how collective mental programming relates to three levels of human mental programming (universal, collective, and individual). He also presents a four-field diagram (1984: 159) showing four cultural dimensions (which later became five) that can be used to distinguish between different cultures. According to Dahlén (1997: 63), these concepts and visuals have become widely cited by consultants:

> These concepts [and visuals] have become part of the vocabulary of interculturalists, despite the fact that many of them have not read Hofstede's book. They know about the concepts from reading other people's books and articles about them, or from having them presented by different speakers.

Hofstede's (1980) original book ran to 476 pages and included source data and statistical proofs and a later abridged version (Hofstede, 1984) of 328 pages still included some statistics, which might have presented an obstacle to reading his book but did not seem to prevent these ideas being referenced and circulated. Indeed, Hofstede is noted as an author with major impact in intercultural communication ahead of Margaret Mead (Harman & Briggs, 1991).

With the forces of globalization of the new millennium, the concept of culture transformed into cosmopolitanism, the ideal of shedding ourselves of our local interests and values and becoming citizens of the world (Zachary, 2000). Cosmopolitanism quickly became a means by which companies could be 'managing culture' and being a cosmopolitan a desirable managerial competence. Queue the management consultants, training manuals, and airport books. Halsall (2009) explores the genre of corporate intercultural training manuals and similar texts that were "[a]rmed with the 'periodic table'" (Holden, 2002, cited in Halsall, 2009: 142) of the cultural dimensional models of Hofstede, amongst others. Within the discourse of this "intercultural training industry" (ibid.: S142), culture was reduced to something out there to be controlled, and the drama of different cultures something to be overcome. Scholars joined the move to categorizing, survey, measure, and evaluate "culture as an independent variable" in the name of management studies (Jack & Westwood, 2009: 35).

Hence, as a carrier of signification, the concept of culture became the way that a group of 'professionals' made themselves. However, for some of these interculturalists (i.e. managers, trainers, consultants) the humanist ethos available in a rich concept (e.g. the potential to enhance cross cultural understandings and relationships) conflicted with market-driven logics and demands. For example, trainers report being torn between wanting to create transformative learning for their participants and the restricted format provided for training alongside the instrumental corporate rationale for engaging intercultural training (Romani & Szkudlarek, 2014).

What can be gleaned from this example of use of the concept of culture in management studies? First, marketization of a concept is reliant on a process of thinning and stabilization, in which simplification, containment, repetition, and visual imagery, inter alia, are key. In the example of culture, we see the rewriting, translation, and approximation of a management concept into a commercial visible and viable product. This process of intervention was enabled by "the conception of culture as something with its own properties, rather tangible, bounded, atemporal, and internally homogeneous" (Dahlen, 1997: 178). This thin stable version of itself, ironically, becomes a trademark of a profession or individual professionals (sometimes literally), thus acting to further reify and freeze the concept despite its contemporaneous evolution in other arenas (e.g. critical anthropology).

Second, and relatedly, commodified concepts carry symbolism to which their purveyors become committed. In the case of culture, the concept was so powerful and contained so much market value that it created a whole industry. However, it did not just create a market; it was also so deep and touching that it created a profession of dedicated self-identifying "interculturalists," a group deeply devoted to faith rather than skepticism (Ricoeur, 1970) as the route to meaning.

The politics of thinning of concepts in management studies

Concepts are not merely used (to understand, explain, predict, and problematize) in management studies; they perform and construct the very knowledge they purportedly seek to explain. Concepts do not merely describe social phenomena; they influence their nature (Sawyer, 2005); they organize and are organizations in themselves (Foucault, 1990).

The cases of the enrollment of justice and culture in management studies, as examples of concept use in management studies, provide further nuance to the procedures of intervention (Foucault, 1990) by which meaning is reduced and stabilized (e.g. simplification, containment, repetition, use of visuals). They bring our attention to the vital role played in concept thinning several factors: the fallacious separation of facts and values; the ignorance of ultimate purposes, that is the marketization of knowledge; and the marketization of the knower.

One can draw a dystopian picture of social scientists who refuse to be philosophers and of concepts severed from their philosophical roots, of a discipline in which concepts are commercializable intellectual products that are used as resources to be traded. In the case of management studies as a form of academic knowledge production, the creators and traders are faculty members at universities and the direct marketplaces are peer-reviewed, listed, and ranked journals. This direct market for academic concepts is linked to a wider indirect market for academic employment: internal markets for promotion, workloads, research funding; or external markets for jobs, research funding, etc. The commodification of concepts is readily understood in the context of the commodification of the university, the establishment of the 'McUniversity' (Parker & Jary, 1995), and the broader and deeper marketization of knowledge (Dey & Steyaert, 2007; Lyotard, 1984). Concepts, like knowledge more broadly, are legitimized by and, in turn, legitimate 'technical' games (efficiency versus inefficient) over denotative games (true versus false) and prescriptive games (just versus unjust) (Lyotard, 1984: 46). Concepts are valued for their capacity to achieve outcomes and generate returns effectively. For management studies, this can almost be reduced to the A* publication hit.

Even so, one might assume there is a philosopher in all of us. A scholar could not be interested in a concept, could not stress concern for that concept, if she did not expect that the concept would 'address' itself to her (Ricoeur, 1970: 29). For Foucault (1990: 9), the purpose of creating one's own history of a concept is to "free thought from what it silently thinks, and so enable it to think differently." Adopting Fleetwood and Ackroyd's (2005: 3) position, previously cited, we would agree that "we cannot gain access to the world independently of the concepts we use," and therefore that we should take concepts as the underpinning practice of our inquiry.

Concept as method: addressing the enriching of method with concepts

The concept of *concept as methods* is a thick concept in many senses, but most of all because at first hearing it creates a new way of thinking. At a personal level for one of the authors, hearing it "produced an immediate and intense rupture that stopped me in my tracks" (St. Pierre, 2017: 686). These three words, which had been spoken individually countless times but rarely in the formation *concept as method,* came as gift.[6] Thus, we gathered our white gloves and dived into the rabbit hole of post-qualitative inquiry (Taguchi & St. Pierre, 2017) from where the concept derived. From this excursion came a thought-experiment to approach qualitative methods from the opposite direction from how management scholars commonly approach these methods (i.e. as a counterpoint to quantitative methods) and use post-qualitative concepts as provocation against 'humanistic' qualitative methods. In a sense, this can be seen an exercise into the limits of a hermeneutics of faith as challenged by a hermeneutics of suspicion, the restoration of meaning through the undoing of meaning. Hence in this section, we explore how we can use concepts to thicken our research methods.

Using 'concept as method' to problematize qualitative research

The legitimation of knowledge based on its utility for technical outcomes sits in opposition to the interests of research (Lyotard, 1984; Woodard, 2018). The role of research is and should be the production of ideas.

This is not to say that knowledge created from our research should not address real and pragmatic problems, on the contrary. However, knowledge produced and legitimized in service of narrow-serving performance goals will result in the perversion and reduction of research. As an alternative, Jean-François Lyotard (1984: 60) posited "legitimation by paralogy." The etymology of paralogy is found in the Greek words para (meaning beside, past, or beyond) and logos (meaning reason). Thus paralogy is "the movement beyond or against reason ... a movement against an established way or reasoning" (Woodard, 2018, n.p.). Rather than search for consensus or appeal to a grand narrative, the point of research in the "post-modern condition" is to seek out instabilities. Lyotard (1984: 100, notes 210 and 211) argues that we should employ locally determined narrative knowledge (as opposed to 'scientific' or abstract knowledge) as a type of 'anti-method' (or 'epistemological anarchism' in terms of Feyerabend, 1993/1975). This emphasis on knowledge as revealing and articulating the unknown, yet arising from problems known to our worlds, is echoed in Colebrook's claim that concepts are in and of themselves methods:

> It is in this respect we might begin to think of concepts as methods, precisely because concepts are at once prehuman (emerging from the problems or plane of thinking in which we find ourselves), but that also reconfigure or reorient the plane precisely by being prompted by a problem. Concepts are methods precisely because they emerge from problems rather than questions.
> (Colebrook, 2017)

Thinking of concept as methods gives us a way to problematize our methods. We need to problematize our methods because we are caught in a cycle of resisting and refining, rather than refusing. We are embroiled in the structures of power that permeate research institutions and practices, and complicit in divisive and problematic practices that lead to subjectification of researchers and the researched (Gerrard, Rudolph, & Sriprakash, 2017; Greenwood, 2016). In the words of Gherardi, (2019: 44) "it is not a matter of looking harder or more closely, but of *seeing what frames our spaces of constructed visibility*, following Derrida's (1978) and Foucault's (1972) lessons to look for what constitutes power/knowledge."

Furthermore, our methods (derived from social science) may be discordant with the motivations of our research (arising from philosophical and political concerns). That is we are confounded by trying to use the sociological methods to address philosophical problems.[7] This potential disconnect, between *philosophical empiricism* that refuses to take as its starting point knowledge of the pre-existing and *social science empiricism* that valorizes precisely what is there, can be explicated in two interrelated ways (Taguchi & St. Pierre, 2017). First, the thinned concepts employed in social sciences research, which differ in type and degree from thick philosophical concepts, overdetermine inquiry through their tendency to organize, consolidate, and represent experience, as noted in the prior section. And second, pre-planned methods that center on the human (hereafter 'I' methods) likewise overdetermine and reduce inquiry, a point taken up herewith.

Three provocations to qualitative inquiry

Disenchantment with qualitative methods across disciplines has given rise to "post-humanist inquiry" and "refusal methodologies" (Gerrard *et al.*, 2017: 391). What might happen to method in post-qualitative inquiry is "not at all clear"; however, we can assume an ongoing process of deconstruction of key elements of method such as 'data,' 'the field,' 'the interview,' 'observation,' and so on (Gherardi, 2019: 45). Drawing on provocations from post-qualitative inquiry, three modes of working against qualitative method are discussed here – method without rules; methods without subjects; and method without a field – which provide challenges for the way in which qualitative researchers think, interview, and conduct cases.

Method without rules or goals: implications for thinking

If method is a "dogmatic image of thought" that is based on representation and follows predetermined set rules and goals, it is unlikely to capture "the moment when the world kicks back" (St. Pierre, 2017: 687). To move beyond limitations to our inquiry we have to inquire without rules and goals, but how do we think without these? There cannot be a 'recipe' for thinking without method; rather (following Jackson, 2017) we sketch out three enabling conditions: (1) thinking without image, (2) bringing the outside in, and (3) seizing a concept.

Thinking without image. Deleuze (1994: 158) critiques the "dogmatic image of thought," by which he means not just thought as representational common sense but also the predetermined rules and goals of thought, thus subsuming what we might refer to as method. The image of thought acts like a productive machine or apparatus of power, a mechanism that orders and controls our thinking (Voss, 2013).

The very way that text is laid out directs and constrains our thinking (Burrell, 1997). In contrast, thought without image is not focused on the pre-existing and fixed, but rather on that which is de-centered and fractured. Jackson's metaphor to describe thought without image as the "rhizomatic weed between the cracks in the paving" is amusingly visual, and reminiscent of the Barthesian term punctum to describe the mistake or disturbance in a photograph (Barthes, 1981). This is the "too strange" that we discard when we seek scientific data (St. Pierre, 2017: 5). It is this disturbance or difference, "that accident which pricks," that speaks to you and captures you (Barthes, 1981: 27; Greenwood, Jack, & Haylock, 2019) to which we must be open. What is needed is a "new image of thought – or rather, a liberation of thought from those images which imprison it" (Deleuze, 1994: xvi–xvii).

Bringing the outside in. If qualitative inquiry puts methods before thought, we need to step outside of method in order to allow thought. In developing "thinking from outside method" outside and inside are not understood as opposites or even two sides of the same coin (Grosz, 1994); rather outside is an assemblage of interfaces that transform inside to outside (Jackson 2017: 667). Thinking is not something we do, but something that happens to us from outside through an imposition (Colebrook, 2002); that is, we think differently when we are imposed open by force, through an encounter, or by chance (Jackson, 2017):

> Following this move(ment), I situate thinking without method as an encounter with the outside, and by doing so, I disturb notions of a pervasive container view of thinking as relying on an image of recognition (i.e., reflection), closed off from the conditions that generate thought. I extend this critique to qualitative research method and its overuse and overreliance as a script, even loosely followed.
> (Jackson, 2017: 667)

Despite disproportionate homage to male philosophers in their writings against qualitative methods, Jackson and colleagues recognize the legacy of feminism in their "project(s) of refusal"; using the words of Grosz (2011: 77) that to "think like a feminist" is "about the generation of new thought, new concepts, as much as if not more than it is about the critique of existing knowledges." More pointedly, Grosz (1994) offers the Mobius strip[8] as a metaphor for thinking about the relationship between body and mind, a metaphor that can be used more generally for thinking about the relationship between outside and inside, interfaces and the fallacy of dualism. The Mobius strip

> provides a way of problematizing and rethinking the relations between the inside and the outside of the subject ... by showing not their fundamental identity or reducibility but the torsion of the one into the other, the passage, vector, or uncontrollable drift of the inside into the outside and the outside into the inside.
>
> (Grosz, 1994: xii)

Seizing your concept. Where humanist methods might refer to "aha" moments, post-qualitative methods speak of a violent imposition on thinking when "the world kicks back" (Jackson, 2017; Taguchi & St. Pierre, 2017: 644, inspired by Barad, 1999: 2). For thinking to be an act of creation, what is needed is an encounter, by chance and by force, to "awaken thought from its natural stupor" (Deleuze, 1994: 139); an intrusion must be inflicted from the outside in (see previous discussion; Jackson, 2017). This violence is an unhinging of empirical internal faculties, our methods of thinking as we know them, perception, memory, imagination, and so on. Through such a force, new faculties can arise, "new faculties that are unanticipated and unregulated by method" (Jackson, 2017: 669). Between the pleasing "aha" moment and the unhinging violent encounter might lie the provoking "conceptual leap," a mysterious phenomenon in qualitative research that generates abstract theoretical ideas from empirical inquiry (Klag & Langley, 2013: 150).

We may not be able to explain the magic in our method but that does not mean we ought not think about it (May, 1994). We may eschew methods as recipe and refuse a deterministically method that has as its aim to "produce" a conceptual leap, but still consider the conditions that might enable a conceptual leap or the process of conceptual leaping (Klag & Langley, 2013). For Jackson (2017: 673), thinking without methods is enabled by "forgetting method, starting in the middle, and being receptive to chance encounters—all of which involve spontaneity." With greater specificity and allowance for directive, Klag and Langley (2013: 149) explore the conditions for conceptual leaps in terms of four dialectic tensions between disciplining influences and liberating influences: deliberation and serendipity; engagement and detachment; between knowing and not knowing; and self-expression and social connection. Similarly, alongside spontaneity comes continuance, living with your research over time, reading closely and with effort, "slow work that requires a very long preparation" (Gerrard *et al.* 2017; St. Pierre, 2017: 4).

Method without subjects: implications for interviewing

Another aspect of refusal of "conventional humanistic methodology" deconstructs the ontological status of human subjectivity. From a post-qualitative inquiry perspective, the individual 'I' is a grossly inadequate depiction of the 'actor' involved in knowledge creation, whether this actor is taken to be the researcher or the researched, or some combination or interaction thereof. Furthermore, limiting empirical analysis to the spoken word refuses attendance to the words that seem "present in their absence" (Mazzei, 2013: 733), that is, the words that were *not uttered* by the research participant presents, those absent, or others involved in the creation of knowledge.

Employing the Deleuzian concept of haecceity – a this-ness or "mode of individuation very different from that of a person, subject, thing, or substance" (Deleuze & Guattari, 1987: 261) – St. Pierre (2017) argues that an individuation not based on humans and objects cannot be captured from individual's lived experience but through thinking with concepts (as discussed in the previous section). In allied work, Mazzei (2013) builds on the concept of a Body without Organs (Deleuze & Guattari, 1987: 4), to proffer a Voice without Organs – "a voice that does not emanate from a singular subject but is produced in an enactment among research-data-participants-theory-analysis" (Mazzei, 2013: 732) – in order to inform analysis of research interviews. She develops a conception of agency as distributed and enacted, such that the voice that would be heard is an assemblage which attends to all humans and the products of their agency and contexts, and which is made and unmade in research and analysis.

By taking as its foundation non-entitic, multiple, situated agency, the concept of a "dissolved or fractured 'I'" (Voss, 2013: 13) provides a corrective to the human subject interview. First, it is a corrective for the privileging of researchers (i.e. their voice, expert knowledge, and status) in objectivist research and the subjectification and disempowerment of participants in such research. Second, it is also a corrective for the purported reification of the human in humanist research, the specious elevation of the human to the ideal subject, or even subject as victim whom the researcher must save (Brewis & Wray-Bliss, 2008; Greenwood, 2016). Rather than the voice from nowhere[9] assumed by objectivist research, or the voice from somewhere assumed by humanist research, we will see in this non-representationalist logic the potential for capturing the voice from everywhere.

This transcendental condition of thought, brought about by disenthrallment with an entitic subject, works in concert with thinking beyond representation (as discussed in the previous section) and deconstruction of the field (discussed in the next section). As important as individual's lived experiences may be, not all knowledge derives from individual's sensations. Without an 'I' in the foreground, whether that be 'researcher,' 'subject,' or 'object,' the field itself, in its whole constructed or fragmented deconstructed glory, can come to the fore, and the ineffable (i.e. moment when "the world kicks back") can be known. Hence in fracturing the 'I,' a wholeness might be found.

Method without a field: implications for studying cases

Suhaib travels from his Western academic life in North America to India each summer to visit his family and do field research. He returns to attend the *Academy of Management* conference where, without fail and yet seemingly unaware, he moves intuitively between what he has just experienced "in the field" (on the streets, from a railway carriage, in a barbers' shop) and his scholarly presentations. For Suhaib's inquiry, the field has no beginning or end. He has always been in the middle of it.

Unlike natural science, where an observational field "does not mean anything to atoms, molecules, and electrons" and therefore is more amenable to procedural rules, in social science an observational field has "specific meaning and relevance structure for the human beings living, acting, and thinking within it" Shultz (1972/1953: 59), including but not limited to researchers and participants. Drawing from Deleuze and Guattari (1987), Mazzei notes that there is no division between a field of reality (what we ask, what our participants tell us, the location, material artifacts), a field of representation (research narratives constructed for the 'data'), and a field of subjectivity (the experiences of participants and researchers); rather these act on each other simultaneously. Deleuze and Guattari used the term assemblages to describe how we are in the world:

> We are no more familiar with scientif-icity than we are with ideology; all we know are assemblages... An assemblage, in its multiplicity, necessarily acts on semiotic flows, material flows, and social flows simultaneously (independently of any recapitulation that may be made of it in a scientific or theoretical corpus).
> (Deleuze & Guattari, 1987: 22–23)

Suhaib has always been part of India and India will always be part of him. His study "began before it began and [he] had always been in the middle if it" (St. Pierre, 2017: 689). The idea of a circumscribed field that the researcher enters and exits (and then reports on) is based on a number of fallacious boundaries related to time, space, subject position, and how we know. The field does not come into being because we study it, we do not leave it when we stop collecting data, our responsibility to our human subjects do not cease when they are no longer participants:

> It's not easy to see things in the middle, rather than looking down on them from above or up at them from below, or from left to right or right to left: try it, you'll see that everything changes.
> (Deleuze & Guattari, 1987: 23)

How then might we conceive of a boundary-less field and a method through which we can explore it from the middle?

Clinical cases have been posed as a heuristic in which the distinction between modes of case research – cases as theory generating, theory testing, and theory elaborating (Ketokivi & Choi, 2014) – can be collapsed and the inquiry process treated holistically and experientially (Freeman, Kujala, & Sachs, 2017). Originally published in 1985 as *Exploring Clinical Methods for Social Research*, Berg and Smith explain in the second edition of this book (1988: 9) that their use of the term clinical was intended to place "the scrutiny of the self in the center stage of social inquiry." The term *clinical* is commonly associated with the medical profession and *clinical cases* with psychiatry, psychology, and psychoanalysis (famously by Freud, 1895). A number of salient features can be drawn from these therapeutic settings: the systematic examination of the practitioner/researcher and the research relationship; the multiple responsibilities embedded in the setting; the necessary participation of other human beings; and the need to be pragmatic (rather than ideological) about methodology (Berg & Smith, 1988).

Definitively, clinical cases arise from practice; they are not an outcome of a planned and methodical attempt to collect researcher-motivated data; rather they are a narration by the researcher of a therapeutic encounter (Willemsen, Della Rosa, & Kegerreis, 2017). They have as their purpose an understanding of 'persons in particular,' but in the context of the whole of their lives, sometimes even generations, and to share this understanding with others, including but not limited to other clinicians. While some draw a harsh line between the uses of clinical cases in medicine and psychiatry and their use in social sciences (Berg & Smith, 1988), organizational theorists have engaged deeply with theories and metatheories of psychoanalysis if not with specific clinical case methods (e.g. Fotaki, Long, & Schwartz, 2012; Gabriel & Carr, 2002).

What appears to be underemphasized in many defenses of clinical case methods, which are generally undertaken subsuming positivist values of rigor and generalizability (Berg & Smith, 1988; Lowman, 1988; Williemsen et al., 2017), are three key affordances of clinical cases. First, clinical material is inseparable from the research material. Gabriel (1999: 51) argues against the accusation of contamination of the clinical material by people's beliefs and motives, that "it makes no sense to talk of contamination of the research material, since the contamination is itself part of this material and the process of contamination is itself what is being investigated."

Second, the researcher is already in the field. As noted, the boundary of the field in space and time is imposed for analytical purposes. The choice of where to start, "inconsistencies and ambiguities that interfere with a straight line plot" and "loose ends," cannot be written out as they are part of the story (Gabriel, 2017: 407). Furthermore, clinical researchers recognize that they are part of the system they seek to understand and change (Lowman, 1988), that they are not in the field in a delineated location or time; rather that the field always existed and will always exist, with and without them.

Third, the reader is integral to the research. Beyond self-understanding, the *raison d'etre* of the case is to report unexpected or unusual findings; a single aberrant case may prompt greater breakthroughs than large numbers of more conventional ones (Gabriel, 2017). However for others to gain understanding, for them to see authenticity and value in a clinical report, readers need to see not only evidence but also how this evidence is arrived at, in particular the researcher's affective experience. Coen (2000: 452) argues for "open case writing" that allows for the unexpected and that gives readers the freedom to generate new ideas; "writers do us greater service by allowing us to inquire with them rather than insisting on what they and/or we already know." Such open writing allows readers to take their place both within and without the phenomena being explored.

The politics of 'concept as method' in management studies

Despite attempts to radicalized qualitative methodologies, many approaches to qualitative research have not escaped the shadows of 'good' science. Many qualitative researchers do not question fundamental aspects of humanistic qualitative methods: identification and respect for human subjects; rules to enhance research credibility and trustworthiness; and conventions around content and presentations of research findings. Since *Sociological Paradigms and Organizational*

Analysis was published in 1979, the diversity and radical possibilities of management and organizational studies have been nurtured and challenged by countless scholars through many media (e.g. the journals *Organization* and *ephemera*, Critical Management Studies conference, and division of the Academy of Management[10]). At the heart of these radical projects were a deep reflexivity regarding the position of the researcher and the relationship to the research; a heightened concern with the research subject and the relationship between the researcher and research subject; and a commitment to analyzing hegemonies and advancing emancipatory goals.

The strategy of 'anti-method' was proposed to subvert research practices early in reflections beyond method in management studies (Morgan, 1983: 33; Wilson, 1983). In support of anti-method, Wilson (1983) argued that the very structures and methods of social science research, through their alignment of knowledge and control, systematically repress and distort the possibility of free and open inquiry. Central to this domination by bureaucracy is the division of labor between researcher and researched that assumes the researcher has greater capacity for reason and/or access to knowledge than those being researched, thus determining a relationship that tends to exploitation or caretaking (Wilson, 1983), wherein the practice of human ethics is rendered to "ethics as 'hurdle'" or "ethics as seeking our silence" (Brewis & Wray-Bliss, 2008: 1524, 1528). In order to radicalize research methods, Wilson proposed that the plausibility of researchers' interpretation should be assessed by the research participants and their peers (as opposed being assessed by other scholars). This ideal (cf. Brewis and Wray-Bliss' "ethics as central warrant") is more accurately characterized as a politically and ethically radical method, rather than anti-method. Given the history of challenging methods within critical management studies, one might expect discussion of anti-methods to be prevalent. However, in one example of a recently published book from highly regarded authors titled "Unconventional methodology in organization and management research" (Bryman & Buchanan, 2018), despite dealing with the newest technologies, most extreme contexts, and most unconventional methods, there appears to be negligible anti-method sentiment.

Explorations in 'anti-methods' or post-qualitative inquiry explicitly seek to create conceptual and methodological pathways that reject purported essentialisms and determinisms contained within humanism, in particular the codification of our knowledge and the centering of the human subject (Gerrard *et al.*, 2017). They imagine a world where concepts write themselves, where knowledge from everywhere is soaked in like liquid into a sponge, where there are no rules, no subjects, no beginnings, no ends, only immersions. However, post-humanistic research is undertaken by humans and is still concerned with human 'subjects.' Someone has written these words, about something, and under some circumstances. That is to say, post-qualitative inquiry per se clearly has the hands of humans with agency and power written all over it and, furthermore, is subject to and creates its own boundaries. To deny this, in the manner adopted by an anti-methods approach, raises important political and ethical considerations. First, that the turn away from predetermined, rule-bound methods exploring participants' experiences toward researcher intuition and affect may re-empower researchers as elite knowers and re-mystify research practices and processes. This would be akin to returning to a philosophy which "trusted in concepts as completely as [it] mistrusted the senses," in which concepts were seen as "a wonderful dowry from some remote wonderland" (Nietzsche, 1968/1901: 220–221 §409). Second, that this turn may once again subjectify and dis-empower research participants such that "'the researched' are at best muted, or at worst left aside." There is a danger that the voice from everywhere mutates into the voice from nowhere. In the words of Gerrard *et al.* (2017: 384):

> Without explicit attention to power and history, the (non)representational logics of post-qualitative inquiry risk operating less as "new" mechanisms for generative and subversive post-humanist research and more as processes of closure and erasure: closed-off from the worlds and people being researched.

To not consider the political and ethical implications of an assumed 'I' – whether this is due to erasure of the 'I' in post-qualitative methods or due to foreclose of the 'I' in traditional qualitative methods – is to risk running roughshod over those who cannot speak. The 'I' must be opened and critiqued but, inevitably, also owned. In the words of Judith Butler (1992: 9) "My position is mine to the extent that 'I'—and I do not shirk from the pronoun—replay and resignify the theoretical positions that have constituted me."

Conclusion

Concepts are fundamental to our understanding of the world. This chapter explores how concepts bring philosophy into management studies and concludes that concepts are simultaneously educative and articulative but also organizing and limiting. Concepts are foundational to both philosophy and social science/management studies; yet scholars on both sides of this apparent divide subscribe to the belief that concepts in philosophy and concepts in social science are fundamentally different creatures. We argue that not all concepts are created equal, but that this variation does not arise from a disciplinary divide, but rather from how concepts are understood and engaged, how concepts are constructed, and how they are used. Concepts can be thick and they can be thinned. They are thinned through numerous processes such as being reified, measured, visualized, and commoditized. To overcome the thinning of concepts in management studies we need to understand the political context in which concepts are constituted and draw on philosophical thinking to thicken them.

Concepts emerge as epistemology; they become a way in which we know and formulate the world. At some point in time they become solidified and when they become solidified they slowly develop an ontological character; they get sedimented, they get institutionalized. As a result we are in danger of forgetting the fact that there was once a time when these concepts did not exist. Concepts emerge very tentatively; many concepts emerge and then, through process that are institutionally driven and power laden, certain concepts will take hold and be embraced by the field. Once they are secured by the field, they start developing their own reality, and challenging them becomes far more difficult. However, we should never lose sight of the fact that, even with regard to the most embedded concepts, concepts should be constantly subject to the same interrogation process that they were at their inception.

Concepts also emerge as method; indeed methods are what stabilizes concepts and make them appear as real. However, if we do not think philosophically, we do not work our concepts into methods such that they imbue meaning and life into each other. When we use stock, standard template methods without sensitivity to our concepts, we reduce and control the very concepts we purport to be developing. Scholars often do not think about their concepts when they deploy their methods; rather they work to conventional recipes, and the profession rewards them for doing so. One way to thicken our concepts is to integrate them with method, such that concepts and methods become inseparable. The philosophical approach is for methods to be infused with concepts. Deploying concepts as methods that are not totally given and not to be taken as they were given is very important because it reserves the possibility that we continue to look at concepts in an interrogative manner all of the time.

Concepts not only emerge as ontology; according to Deleuze, their role is to "intervene ontologically in the world, and *through this* intervention create something interesting, remarkable, or important" (Kristensen et al., 2014: 499). We create the world in the manner in which we conceive it. In the words of Nietzsche (1968/1901: 282, §521, emphasis added), "One should not understand this compulsion to construct concepts ... as if they enabled us to fix the real world; but as a compulsion *to arrange a world for ourselves in which our existence is made possible.*" In a time in which questions about the possibilities of our existence are so urgent, we cannot afford to take other than a philosophical approach to management concepts.

Notes

1 Bacharach did not differentiate between concepts and constructs; this is our extrapolation.
2 The modifier 'tend' is used here to deliberately avoid the controversial arena of the fact-value distinction (i.e. the notion that this is such a thing as a value-free fact; see Putnam, 2002). While we do not subscribe to this distinction we are suggesting, non-controversially we hope, that some concepts primarily provide descriptive functions and others primarily evaluative functions.
3 Lyotard (1984) used the term *performativity* to describe the search for performance and the formation of knowledge in service thereof. As we use the term performativity somewhat differently in this chapter (see endnote 1) we will adhere to the more prosaic 'technical claims' or 'utility' in discussion of Lyotard's view on the legitimation of knowledge.
4 In this article published in the highly ranked journal *Organizational Studies* the authors use the term 'organizational,' whereas in their article published in the *British Journal of Management* they use the term 'management,' potentially in compliance with the norms of the journals or, more cynically, market demands.
5 Geert Hofstede, originally trained as a social psychologist, became professor of business administration in the mid-1980s and describes himself as an organizational anthropologist, published the highly influential book *Culture's Consequences* in 1980/4.
6 This rupture is marked by the moment when Silvia Gherardi spoke the words "concept as method" during her keynote address at the Gender Work and Organization conference in Sydney 2018.
7 We are indebted to Gavin Jack for this specific insight and to him and our colleagues from CROS (Critical Reorientations of Organisation and Society research group, Monash Business School) for their nurturing of all ideas critical.
8 The Möbius strip is described by Grosz (1994) as an inverted three-dimensional figure that shows the inflection of inside into outside and how, through twisting or inversion, one side becomes the other.

9 This is a play on the idea of the view from nowhere, Nagel's (1986) postulation that objectivist research is characterised and limited by the idea that the researcher can come unencumbered, without assumptions or values, to the field.
10 Ephemera can be found at www.ephemerajournal.org/ Organization can be found at https://journals.sagepub.com/home/org International CMS can be found at https://internationalcms.org/ CMS division of AOM can be found at https://cms.aom.org/home.

References

Abrahamson, E. (1991). Managerial fads and fashions: The diffusion and rejection of innovations. *Academy of Management Review*, 16(3), 586–612.
Abrahamson, E., & Fairchild, G. (1999). Management fashion: Lifecycles, triggers, and collective learning processes. *Administrative Science Quarterly*, 44(4), 708–740.
Alvesson, M., & Sandberg, J. (2011). Generating research questions through problematization. *Academy of Management Review*, 36(2), 247–271.
Bacchi, C. (2015). The turn to problematization: Political implications of contrasting interpretive and poststructural adaptations. *Open Journal of Political Science*, 5, 1–12.
Bacharach, S. B. (1989). Organizational theories: Some criteria for evaluation. *Academy of Management Review*, 14(4), 496–515.
Banks, G. C., Gooty, J., Ross, R. L., Williams, C. E., & Harrington, N. T. (2018). Construct redundancy in leader behaviors: A review and agenda for the future. *The Leadership Quarterly*, 29(1), 236–251.
Barad, K. (1999). Agential realism: Feminist interventions in understanding scientific practices. In M. Biagioli (Ed.), *The science studies reader* (pp. 1–11). New York, NY: Routledge.
Barthes, R. (1981). *Camera Lucida: Reflections on photography* (1st American ed.). New York: Hill and Wang.
Bauman, Z. (1991). *Modernity and ambivalence*. Cambridge, UK: Polity Press.
Benders, J., & Van Veen, K. (2001). What's in a fashion? Interpretative viability and management fashions. *Organization*, 8(1), 33–53.
Berg, D. N., & Smith, K. K. (1988). *The self in social inquiry: Researching methods*. Newbury Park, CA: Sage.
Bies, R. J. (2005). Are procedural justice and interactional justice conceptually distinct? In J. Greenberg & J. A. Colquitt (Eds.), *Handbook of organizational justice* (pp. 85–112). Mahwah, NJ: Lawrence Erlbaum Associates.
Bort, S., & Kieser, A. (2011). Fashion in organization theory: An empirical analysis of the diffusion of theoretical concepts. *Organization Studies*, 32(5), 655–681.
Brewis, J., & Wray-Bliss, E. (2008). Re-searching ethics: Towards a more reflexive critical management studies. *Organization Studies*, 29(12), 1521–1540. doi:10.1177/0170840607096385.

Bryman, A., & Buchanan, D. A. (2018). *Unconventional methodology in organization and management research.* Oxford: Oxford University Press.

Burrell, G. (1997). *Pandemonium: Towards a retro-organization theory.* London: Sage.

Butler, J. (1992). Contingent foundations: Feminism and the question of "postmodernism". In J. Butler & J. W. Scott (Eds.), *Feminists theorize the political* (pp. 3–21). New York: Routledge.

Clegg, S., Kornberger, M., & Rhodes, C. (2007). Organizational ethics, decision making, undecidability. *The Sociological Review, 55*(2), 393–409.

Coen, S. J. (2000). Why we need to write openly about our clinical cases. *Journal of the American Psychoanalytic Association, 48*(2), 449–470.

Colebrook, C. (2002). *Understanding Deleuze.* Crows Nest, NSW, Australia: Allen & Unwin.

Colebrook, C. (2017). What is this thing called Education? *Qualitative Inquiry, 23*(9), 649–655.

Cummings, S., Bridgman, T., Hassard, J., & Rowlinson, M. (2017). *A new history of management.* Cambridge: Cambridge University Press.

Dahlén, T. (1997). *Among the interculturalists: An emergent profession and its packaging of knowledge.* (PhD dissertation), Stockholm University, Stockholm.

Deleuze, G. (1994). *Difference and repetition.* New York: Columbia University Press.

Deleuze, G., & Guattari, F. (1987). *A thousand plateaus: Capitalism and schizophrenia* (B. Massumi, Trans.). Minneapolis, MN: University of Minnesota Press.

Deleuze, G., & Guattari, F. (1994). *What is philosophy?* (H. Tomlinson & G. Burchell, Trans.). New York: Columbia University Press.

Derrida, J. (1978/1967). *Writing and difference* (A. Bass, Trans.). Chicago, IL: University of Chicago Press.

Dey, P., & Steyaert, C. (2007). The troubadours of knowledge: Passion and invention in management education. *Organization, 14*(3), 437–461.

Elkington, J. (2018). 25 years ago I coined the phrase "triple bottom line." Here's why it's time to rethink it. *Harvard Business Review.* Retrieved from https://hbr.org/2018/06/25-years-ago-i-coined-the-phrase-triple-bottom-line-heres-why-im-giving-up-on-it

Feyerabend, P. (1993/1975). *Against method.* London: Verso.

Fleetwood, S., & Ackroyd, S. (2005). Editors' introduction: Critical realist applications in organisation and management studies. In S. Fleetwood & S. Ackroyd (Eds.), *Critical realist applications in organisation and management studies* (pp. 1–5). London: Routledge.

Fortin, M., & Fellenz, M. R. (2008). Hypocrisies of fairness: Towards a more reflexive ethical base in organizational justice research and practice. *Journal of Business Ethics, 78*(3), 415–433.

Fotaki, M., Long, S., & Schwartz, H. S. (2012). What can psychoanalysis offer organization studies today? Taking stock of current developments and thinking about future directions. *Organization Studies, 33*(9), 1105–1120.

Foucault, M. (1972). *Archaeology of knowledge* (A. M. S. Smith, Trans.). New York: Pantheon Books.
Foucault, M. (1990). *The history of sexuality, vol. 2: The use of pleasure*. New York: Vintage.
Freeman, R. E., Kujala, J., & Sachs, S. (2017). *Stakeholder engagement: Clinical research cases*. Cham, Switzerland: Springer.
Freud, S., & Breuer, J. (2004 (1895)). *Studies in hysteria*. London: Penguin.
Friedrichsen, G. W. S., & Onions, C. T. (1973). *The shorter Oxford English dictionary on historical principles*: Oxford: Clarendon Press.
Gabriel, Y. (1999). *Organizations in depth: The psychoanalysis of organizations*. London: Sage.
Gabriel, Y. (2017). Case studies as narratives: Reflections prompted by the case of Victor, the wild child of Aveyron. *Journal of Management Inquiry, 28*(4), 403–408.
Gabriel, Y., & Carr, A. (2002). Organizations, management and psychoanalysis: An overview. *Journal of Managerial Psychology, 17*(5), 348–365.
Gerrard, J., Rudolph, S., & Sriprakash, A. (2017). The politics of post-qualitative inquiry: History and power. *Qualitative inquiry, 23*(5), 384–394.
Gherardi, S. (2019). If we practice posthumanist research, do we need 'gender'any longer? *Gender, Work & Organization, 26*(1), 40–53.
Green, J., & Thorogood, N. (2018). *Qualitative methods for health research*. UK: Sage.
Greenwood, M. (2016). Approving or improving research ethics in management journals. *Journal of Business Ethics, 137*(3), 507–520.
Greenwood, M., & Van Buren, H. J. (2017). Ideology in HRM scholarship: Interrogating the ideological performativity of 'New Unitarism'. *Journal of Business Ethics, 142*(4), 663–678.
Greenwood, M., Jack, G., & Haylock, B. (2019). Toward a methodology for analyzing visual rhetoric in corporate reports. *Organizational Research Methods, 22*(3), 798–827. doi:10.1177/1094428118765942.
Grosz, E. (2011). *Becoming undone: Darwinian reflections on life, politics, and art*. Durham, NC: Duke University Press.
Grosz, E. A. (1994). *Volatile bodies: Toward a corporeal feminism*. Bloomington IN: Indiana University Press.
Halsall, R. (2009). The discourse of corporate cosmopolitanism. *British Journal of Management, 20*, S136–S148.
Harman, R. C., & Briggs, N. E. (1991). SIETAR survey: Perceived contributions of the social sciences to intercultural communication. *International Journal of Intercultural Relations, 15*(1), 19–28.
Hirsch, P. M., & Levin, D. Z. (1999). Umbrella advocates versus validity police: A life-cycle model. *Organization science, 10*(2), 199–212.
Hofstede, G. H. (1980). *Culture's consequences: International differences in work-related values*. Beverly Hills, CA: Sage Publications.
Hofstede, G. H. (1984). *Culture's consequences: International differences in work-related values*. Beverly Hills, CA: Sage Publications.

Jack, G., & Westwood, R. (2009). *International and cross-cultural management studies: A postcolonial reading*. Basingstoke, UK: Palgrave McMillilan.

Jackson, A. Y. (2017). Thinking without method. *Qualitative Inquiry, 23*(9), 666–674.

Jackson, N., & Carter, P. (2007). Workers of the world relax! Introducing a philosophy of idleness to organisational studies. In C. Jones & R. ten Bos (Eds.), *Philosophy and organization* (pp. 143–156). Abingdon, Oxon: Routledge.

Jones, C., & ten Bos, R. (2007). Introduction. In C. Jones & R. ten Bos (Eds.), *Philosophy and organization* (pp. 1–17). Abingdon, Oxon: Routledge.

Ketokivi, M., & Choi, T. (2014). Renaissance of case research as a scientific method. *Journal of Operations Management, 32*(5), 232–240.

Klag, M., & Langley, A. (2013). Approaching the conceptual leap in qualitative research. *International Journal of Management Reviews, 15*(2), 149–166.

Kristensen, A. R., Lopdrup-Hjorth, T., & Sørensen, B. M. (2014). Gilles Deleuze (1925–1995). In J. Helin, T. Hernes, D. Hjorth, & R. Holt (Eds.), *The Oxford handbook of process philosophy and organization studies*. www.oxfordhandbooks.com/view/10.1093/oxfordhb/9780199669356.001.0001/oxfordhb-9780199669356-e-031.

Lowman, R. L. (1988). What is clinical method? In D. N. B. K. K. Smith (Ed.), *The self in social inquiry* (pp. 173–187). Newbury Park, CA: Sage.

Lyotard, J. F. (1984). *The postmodern condition: A report on knowledge*. Manchester: Manchester University Press.

May, K. A. (1994). Abstract knowing: The case for magic in method. In J. M. Mors (Ed.), *Critical issues in qualitative research* (pp. 10–21). Thousand Oaks, CA: Sage Publications.

Mazzei, L. A. (2013). A voice without organs: Interviewing in posthumanist research. *International Journal of Qualitative Studies in Education, 26*(6), 732–740.

Mir, R., Willmott, H., & Greenwood, M. (2016). Philosophy in organization studies: Life, knowledge and disruption. In R. Mir, H. Willmott, & M. Greenwood (Eds.), *The Routledge companion to philosophy in organization studies* (pp. 1–11). Abingdon, UK: Routledge.

Morgan, G. (1983). *Beyond method: Strategies for social research*. Beverly Hills, CA: Sage.

Nagel, T. (1986) *The view from nowhere*. Oxford: Oxford University Press.

Nietzsche, F. W. (1954/1873). On truth and lie in an extra-moral sense. In W. Kaufmann (Ed.), *The Portable Nietzsche* (pp. 42–47). New York: Viking Press.

Nietzsche, F. W. (1968/1901). *The will to power* (W. Kaufmann & R. J. Hollingdale, Trans.). New York: Vintage.

Osigweh, C. A. B. (1989). Concept fallibility in organizational science. *Academy of Management Review, 14*(4), 579–594.

Parker, M., & Jary, D. (1995). The McUniversity: Organization, management and academic subjectivity. *Organization, 2*(2), 319–338.

Phillips, R., Freeman, R. E., & Wicks, A. C. (2003). What stakeholder theory is not. *Business Ethics Quarterly, 13*(4), 479–502.

Putnam, H. (2002). *The collapse of the fact/value dichotomy and other essays*. Cambridge, MA: Harvard University Press.

Rhodes, C. H. (2016). Justice: Re-membering the Other in organization. In R. Mir, Willmott, H. & M. Greenwood (Ed.), *The Routledge companion to philosophy in organization studies*. London: Routledge.

Ricoeur, P. (1970). *Freud and philosophy: An essay on interpretation*. New Haven, CT: Yale University Press.

Romani, L., & Szkudlarek, B. (2014). The struggles of the interculturalists: Professional ethical identity and early stages of codes of ethics development. *Journal of Business Ethics*, *119*(2), 173–191.

Sawyer, A. (2005). Foreward: Why critical realism? In S. Fleetwood & S. Ackroyd (Eds.), *Critical realist applications in organisation and management studies* (pp. 6–20). London: Routledge.

Schutz, A. (1972/1953). *Collected papers I. The problem of social reality*. Dordrecht, Netherlands: Springer.

Searle, J. (1964). How to derive "ought" from "is". *Philosophical Review 73*(1), 43–58.

St. Pierre, E. A. (2017). Haecceity: Laying out a plane for post qualitative inquiry. *Qualitative Inquiry*, *23*(9), 686–698.

Starbuck, W. H. (2009). The constant causes of never-ending faddishness in the behavioral and social sciences. *Scandinavian Journal of Management*, *25*(1), 108–116.

Suddaby, R. (2010). Editor's comments: Construct clarity in theories of management and organization. *Academy of Management Review*, *35*(3), 346–357.

Taguchi, H. L., & St. Pierre, E. A. (2017). Using concept as method in educational and social science inquiry. *Qualitative Inquiry*, *23*(9), 643–648. doi:10.1177/1077800417732634.

Väyrynen, P. (2017). Thick ethical concepts. In E. N. Zalta (Ed.), *The Stanford encyclopedia of philosophy* (Fall 2017 ed.). Stanford, CA: Metaphysics Research Lab, Stanford University. Retrieved from <https://plato.stanford.edu/archives/fall2017/entries/thick-ethical-concepts/>.

Voss, D. (2013). *Conditions of thought*. Edinburgh, UK: Edinburgh University Press.

Willemsen, J., Della Rosa, E., & Kegerreis, S. (2017). Clinical case studies in psychoanalytic and psychodynamic treatment. *Frontiers in Psychology*, *8*(108), 1–7.

Wilson, H. T. (1983). Anti-method as counter structure in social research practice. In G. Morgan (Ed.), *Beyond method: Strategies for social research* (pp. 247–259). Beverly Hills, CA: Sage.

Woodard, A. (2018). Jean-François Lyotard. *The internet encyclopedia of philosophy, ISSN 2161-0002*, www.iep.utm.edu/, 12th July 2018.

Zachary, G. P. (2000). *The global me: New cosmopolitans and the competitive edge: Picking globalism's winners and losers*. New York, NY: Nicholas Brealey Publishing.

3 Philosophy from below

In the words of Karl Marx, "Philosophers have hitherto only *interpreted* the world in various ways; the point is to *change* it" (1998 [1888]: 227, original emphasis). It is one of the most fundamental tasks of critical philosophers to develop and analyze ways in which our understanding of the world intersects with the world of praxis. One way to do it is to understand social and work-based relationships through the perspective of power, of dominance, and of resistance. In this chapter, we do so by conceptualizing the world of management and organizational philosophy from the viewpoint of those who occupy a subaltern position in power-laden arrangements, in society, and in the world of organizations and work.

Given the magisterial power of Marx and the hegemonic sway of his analysis of class conflict in society, it is only natural that most critiques of the structural ways in which oppression occurs in capitalist society must travel by way of the great theorist (Marens & Mir, 2016). But does being true to Marx mean being hostile to philosophy? Critics of a philosophical approach to social issues have sometimes used Marx's ringing words quoted above, constituting the entirety of his *Eleventh Thesis on Feuerbach* (Marx, 1998/1888), to develop a dichotomy between philosophy (the act of 'interpreting' the world) and social theory and activism (the 'changing' of the world, or the study of how it can be 'changed'). It has been our contention in this book that such a dichotomy is spurious and often disingenuous. We argue for a nuanced reading of the Eleventh Thesis. Marx's pronouncement therein must be read more as a rhetorical flourish, a critique of those thinkers who choose not to engage with the material conditions in which society and humanity are imbedded, rather than a repudiation of philosophy.

Marx provides but one among several entry points into our understanding of philosophy from below. Other perspectives are not as focused on class conflict as the Marxian approach, but come to it from different cultural and identity-based positions. For instance, feminist philosophers have constantly reminded us that the male perspective is represented in traditional philosophy as a referent and the female position as a lack, thereby providing a male-centric view of the world (de Beauvoir, 1957/ 1988). Researchers, philosophers, and activists from the Global South have continually critiqued theorists from the Metropolitan North for representing their own histories as generalized theoretical referents (Loomba, 2007). Queer theorists often point to *heteronormativity*, the problematic practice of representing non-heterosexual positions as deviant despite constant evidence of the diversity of sexual identity and practice in society (Butler, 2011). It behooves the critical philosopher therefore to imagine the converse, and visualize or construct alternate worlds where the female, queer, non-White, and other marginalized positions are viewed as epistemologically and ontologically legitimate. The marginalized position needs to be honored, and accorded the position of *theory* rather than a putatively innate *identity* or *culture*, if we are to be democratic in our philosophical outlook.

It is our intention in this chapter to present a quick review of the philosophical underpinnings of those who represent marginalized subjectivities. Such a review is bound to be fleeting, contingent, and riddled with omissions, given our space constraints. Our hope is to provide enough information for the reader to be better acquainted with a few strands of philosophy from below, should they choose to examine how philosophical agency can be restored to subjects that had hitherto been confined to the shadows of the social sciences theory in general and management theory in particular.

In this chapter,[1] we offer six strands of philosophy from below. First we discuss the philosophical underpinnings of the class-based analysis of society and work, where the positions of workers engaged in class conflict with their bosses are highlighted as a case of neo-realist and post-realist epistemologies. Second, we examine feminist philosophy as a case of epistemic decentering, where the philosopher can 'change the subject' and accord agency to marginalized subjectivities through the philosophical decentering of male referents. Third, we study the phenomenon of postcoloniality as a constructivist philosophical approach, which sees traditional philosophy as being willfully complicit in the ideological exclusion of non-Western subjectivities. Fourth, we examine the Subaltern Studies movement as a neo-Gramscian philosophical approach, one where the sociocultural superstructure is visualized as being free of the economic base, relatively autonomous and non-deterministic in character. Fifth, we study the phenomenon of political society (as opposed to civil society) as a case of critical realism in action. Finally, we review critical transnationalism as an example of reflexive ontology, as yet another exemplar of philosophy from below.

The philosophy of class conflict

A fair warning must be offered; the name of Karl Marx is writ large on our analysis of the philosophical underpinnings of class conflict. Marx has been quoted and analyzed more than most Western theorists; the historian Gertrude Himmelfarb went so far as to complain that "we are all Marxists now" (Himmelfarb, 1989: 34). The reason for that is itself a tribute; Marx's prescient understanding of social class, the emergence and subsequent dominance of capitalism as a mode of production, and the contradictions that it embodied make it easy and useful to develop our analysis through a Marxian lens. His exhortation of workers to unite against its depredations and subsequent analyses of social relations through a lens of class conflict that were conducted as an extension of his work provide several templates for philosophical analysis. It also helps that Marx himself was a philosopher, whatever disdain he may have rhetorically exhibited through the epigraph above. His paradigmatic work *Das Kapital* (Marx, 1865/2018) remains a marvel of careful philosophizing. According to the French philosopher Étienne Balibar,

> the most technical arguments of Capital are also those in which the categories of logic and ontology, the representations of the individual and the social bond, were wrested from their traditional definitions and re-thought in terms of the necessities of historical analysis.
>
> (Balibar, 2014: 5)

Marx's idea of the world was fundamentally aligned with a view of reality as socially constructed. Marxist approaches have always been "ontologically reflexive, epistemologically dynamic and methodologically heterodox, the very definition of a philosophical approach" (Marens & Mir, 2016: 147). However, there have been theorists who have shunned a reflexive epistemological and ontological position, preferring the 'solidity' of realism while understanding the way in which social arrangements become modes of structural oppression (Miliband, 1969). Such thinkers often (in our view erroneously) assume the mantle of 'true Marxists,' viewing their more reflexive colleagues and their positions as 'relativist.' Marxism however, traverses a broader spectrum, and includes ideas that are culturally and politically anchored as well, as represented by the works of the Italian theorist Antonio Gramsci (1954/1992), the Martinique-based revolutionary Frantz Fanon (Fanon, 1961), and a host of others.

However, many theorists of class formation and class conflict adhere to realist, critical-realist, as well as more reflexive epistemologies (Marxism is fundamentally anti-positivist). One good example of a realist analysis of class conflict is Katherine Stone's *The Origins of Job Structures in the Steel Industry* (Stone, 1974). Using archival analysis, Stone demonstrates how American steel workers were systematically deskilled, not by some external technological determinism or spontaneously occurring innovation, but by managerial action, which included strike-fomenting, strike-breaking, and subsequent regimes of accommodation and intimidation.

Moving a bit further towards reflexivity, labor process theorists like Harry Braverman and Michal Burawoy studied the workplace as a contested terrain, where division of labor, deskilling, and technological deployment was used to secure the partial consent of workers in the workplace of the late twentieth century (Braverman, 1974; Burawoy, 1979; see Knights & Willmott, 2016 for a comprehensive analysis). Organizational philosophers understood organizational elements as a *dialectic practice* (Benson, 1977), bringing Marx's ideas of *historical materialism* into the organizational realm. The core concepts of historical materialism included surplus value, exploitation, class struggle, alienation, contradiction, and ideology (Prasad, 2017: 113–135).

Marxism as a political philosophy suffered a decline in legitimacy in the 1980s and 1990s because it was perceived to be related to the economic policies of the Soviet Union. The fall of the Berlin Wall and the subsequent breakup of the USSR seemed to have struck the death-knell of Marxism, in the eyes of its triumphalist interlocutors. However, in the aftermath of the financial crisis of 2008, the idea of Marxism rose anew, with many analysts suggesting that it had emerged as the best theory to analyze the crises of capitalism and potential responses to them (Prichard & Mir, 2010). Of course, Marxism had to be rescued from the many illiberal socio-political institutions that had committed excesses in its name. We needed a new Marxist *philosophy,* one that emphasized its humanitarian and compassionate elements, and framed it as essentially anti-positivist (Balibar, 2014).

Despite its philosophical reflexivity, Marxist analysis of class continues to struggle with the assumption that it is economically deterministic, i.e. that Marx saw all sociocultural phenomena as a reflection of the economic base. It was left to later Marxists such as the French philosopher Louis Althusser to develop a theory of *overdetermination,* explaining that culture, state-level actions, and ideology are more autonomous, and that the power of the economy in determining them is exercised only "in the last instance" Althusser (1965/2005). Ideology, or the universalization of elite interests as the interests of the whole, remains a powerful tool of class analysis, and in management theory functions to align the field towards the interests of top management. Philosophy from below attempts to rectify such hegemony.

Changing the subject: the case of feminist philosophy

The idea of equality between the sexes must be as old as political thought itself, but ironically, the term *feminism* is credited to a man. The French philosopher Charles Fourier is believed to have coined the term in the mid-nineteenth century. The principles of feminism had of course already been articulated by women before that moment, as far back as the eighteenth century (Wollstonecraft, 1792/1992). The 'second wave' of feminist theory that emerged in the twentieth century, linking back to the French philosopher Simone de Beauvoir, whose contention that "one is not born, but rather becomes, a woman" (Beauvoir, 1957/1988: 295), inaugurated a consciously philosophical assertion that *gender* was ultimately a social construction.

"Feminism is the radical notion that women are people..." The dripping irony evident in the words of the activist/academic Cheris Kramarae perhaps best represents the important work of the second-wave feminists (Kramarae, 1992). They cemented the idea within all conversations that the exclusion of women from the echelons of power was unrepresentative, unethical, and untenable. More importantly, from a philosophical point of view, they demonstrated that even when one was talking about seemingly gender-neutral issues, the constructs being used were male-referential. In the context of organizational studies, we could say that when we spoke of 'leadership' or 'innovation' or 'strategy' or any such concept, we needed to acknowledge that our understanding of the concept was fundamentally gendered and needed unpacking.

Feminism has been subjected to many a philosophical analysis (see Benhabib, 1995 for one among several reviews), and has been analyzed as a philosophy by a variety of management theorists as well (Calás, Smircich, & Holvino, 2014). Feminist theories almost by definition subscribe to a philosophy-from-below approach; women workers have always struggled for equality in the workplace. From the early articulations of "women in management," theorists have used philosophy-based approaches to argue for gender equality in the realm of work (Valian, 1999). A more critical philosophical approach centered upon the constitution and subsequent critique of the non-essential but power-laden construct of *patriarchy*.

In opposition to patriarchy, radical feminists often highlighted gender differences in an example of contingent realism, arguing that the act of reifying gender differences and advocating for a female-centric philosophy could offer the potential of gender solidarity unencumbered by male referents. In the world of organizations, Kathy Ferguson's book *The Radical Case Against Bureaucracy* suggested that organizations were inherently patriarchal spaces (Ferguson, 1984). Socialist feminists were more critical-realist in their epistemological outlook, casting the excessive exploitation of women relative to men as a particular instance of class oppression that patriarchal Marxists had overlooked (Acker, 2006). From a philosophical standpoint, most feminists chose constructivist approaches, decentering patriarchy as a formulation that could be overcome through feminist innovations, and occasionally a re-imagining (Gibson-Graham, 1995). Operating at the intersection of philosophy and psychoanalysis, theorists attempted to revisit theories of the self, and scrub them free of patriarchal assumptions about behavior, sexuality, and communal practices (Gilligan, 1982).

As feminist philosophy became more legitimate, it was natural that it spawned an internal dialogue about the nature of woman as an ontological referent and feminist theorizing as epistemic practice. In particular, postcolonial feminists argued for even more ontological diversity, where the female referent was freed from a Western archetype, rescuing non-White women from the condition of having to operate "under Western eyes" (Mohanty, 1988). In a sense, postcolonial feminists pointed an accusatory finger at liberal feminism, implying that it was proto-patriarchal in the way it attempted to 'save' brown women without demonstrating empathy for their contexts. In many ways, the construct of 'heteronormativity' developed by queer theorists has a lot in common with postcolonial feminists, with both of them calling out hidden referents that elided their realities and fixed them in time and space.

To summarize, the core concepts of feminist philosophy include the idea of gender (and even sex) as a social construction; patriarchy as a structural source of oppression that is open to dialectical contestation; an examination of the deployment of gender in work practices such as the gendered division of labor; sexuality as a produced construct that embodies routines of control; and issues of the invisibility of women in mainstream philosophical tradition.

Postcoloniality as a case of critical constructivism

At its heart, colonialism is just a special case of exploitation.

Consider, for example, a quote quoted above from an almost 200-year-old tract by Lord Thomas Macaulay that provides an insight into the manner in which colonial powers used certain institutions to further their power. Titled 'A Minute on Indian Education,' the piece became the basis of British educational policy in India, one that turned a facility in English into a marker of privilege (Macaulay, 1835/1972), a cultural politics that continues to hold sway in contemporary South Asia. He said:

> We must at present do our best to form a class who may be interpreters between us and the millions we govern; a class of persons, Indian in blood and colour, but English in taste, in opinions, in morals, and in intellect. To that class, we may leave it to refine the vernacular dialects of the country, to enrich those dialects with terms of science borrowed from the western nomenclature, and to render them by degrees fit vehicles for conveying knowledge to the great mass of population.

Similar colonial pronouncements were made and policies enacted in other colonized spaces such as Egypt or Nigeria. As Macaulay's Minute highlights, these policies were themselves predicated upon a variety of racist assumptions about the 'nature' of the native population (for a detailed discussion of Macaulay's racism, see Rajan, 1999), and were sedimented within mainstream social theory (often because they became self-fulfilling prophecies), re-emerging as old wine in new bottles in the postcolonial period in the form of 'modernization theory.'

The quote from Macaulay is instructive because it points to two significant realities. First, it laid the groundwork for a variety of institutional changes in the Indian educational system. As Homi Bhabha (1984) has noted, many of the institutions that were established in the colonies by governing powers were aimed towards making the population more governable and more 'understandable' by the colonizing elites. This desire to better understand the natives was of course meant to serve the purpose of a more efficient exploitation of the colonies. Second, the creation of the "class of persons, Indian in blood and colour, but English in taste" – essentially a comprador native elite – was a result of Macaulay's intervention. This Anglicized native elite was characterized by both an internalization of colonial attitudes towards the vast majority of the Indian population, and a gradual rejection of colonial overlordship fueled by the realization that to the Englishman, they would always remain 'wogs' and 'brown sahibs' (see Fanon, 1967 and Nandy, 1983 for nuanced psychoanalytic readings of this phenomenon).

Much of the colonized world achieved formal political decolonization in the wake of World War II. The project of 'epistemological decolonization' was to prove more elusive. The erstwhile colonies found themselves mired in a neocolonial world order, in which their formal colonial masters continued to hold the economic and political cards in a rigged game. Colonial policy re-emerged as 'development policy,' and colonial tropes found new life within 'modernization theory,' the better to govern the 'Third World' with. The dominant logic of these new modes of governance and extraction can be seen at work in this communiqué from the United Nations (UN) Department of Economic Affairs in 1951 (quoted in Escobar, 1995:3):

> There is a sense in which rapid economic progress is impossible without painful adjustments. Ancient philosophies have to be scrapped; old social institutions have to disintegrate; bonds of caste, creed and race have to burst; and large numbers of persons who cannot keep up with progress will have to have their expectations of a comfortable life frustrated.

As Escobar demonstrates in his detailed readings of UN actions in the 1950s and 1960s, development economists in the UN were determined to 'free' natives from their culture, regardless of how painful this might prove to be. Of course, the modernity that the natives were to be ushered into was to be a capitalist one. This is significant given that modernization theory and the development project it gave birth to were a product of the Cold War, and designed explicitly as a counter to the Soviet model of economic growth (Makki, 2004). The response of the former colonies to this approach was complicated and varied, given that the paternalism embedded within modernization theory was often shared by the former 'brown and black sahibs,' now in power in these newly independent nations of the Third World. This early period of the Cold War was one characterized by contentiousness. A critical Third World social scientific scholarship and scholarly community soon emerged, deeply inflected by varieties of Marxism, and focused on theorizing the contemporary period of postcolonial independence as one of neo-colonialism/neo-imperialism. Some key examples of this scholarship were the Latin American Dependencia school, the Marxist sociology of the Pakistani sociologist Hamza Alavi, and the work of Indian historian D.D. Kosambi. In recent years, organizational theorists have critiqued the paradigm of development management as well (Dar &

Cooke, 2008), especially with regard to the regimes of surveillance, control they deploy in managing their operations in poorer countries, and their Eurocentric assumptions.

The publication of Edward Said's book *Orientalism* in 1978 is broadly accepted as being a critical event for postcolonial studies. Of course, a pre-history of postcolonialism had long been rooted in what we now refer to as the anti-colonial tradition. As Prasad (2003: 7) asserts, postcolonialism "needs to be seen as building upon the contributions of a number of earlier thinkers, freedom fighters and anticolonial activists" such as Guinea-Bissau's Amílcar Cabral, Martinique's Aimé Césaire, the Martinique-born French-Algerian Frantz Fanon, India's Mahatma Gandhi, Vietnam's Ho Chi Minh, Zambia's Kenneth Kaunda, Kenya's Jomo Kenyatta, Russia's Vladimir Lenin, Congo's Patrice Lumumba, Peru's José Carlos Mariátegui, Madagascar's Octave Mannoni, Tunisia's Albert Memmi, Ghana's Kwame Nkrumah, Tanzania's Julius Nyerere, and Senegal's Léopold Sédar Senghor, among others.

Said's contribution was novel in two ways. First, he was able to conduct a meticulous genealogical analysis of various orientalist works of the time and highlight how they manufactured a certain sort of eastern creature (e.g. 'the lustful Turk') that had much more to say about those researchers than the region they purported to illuminate. Second, he was able to highlight how even liberal and class-conscious Westerners (e.g. Albert Camus) treated oriental subjects as people without history. For example, he analyzed Camus' famous novels like *The Stranger* and *The Plague*, and reflected on how Arabs were treated in these works as people without history: "...true, Meursault kills an Arab, but this Arab is not named and seems to be without a history, let alone a mother and father; true also, Arabs die of plague in Oran, but they are not named either" (Said, 1978: 175).

Postcolonial theorists sought to highlight the continued impact of colonialism in the now-independent former colonies. They produce a linkage between the violence visited upon colonial subjects and the representation of the erstwhile colonies in the Western world. They sought the dignity of labels like *theory* for anti-colonial struggles, rather than the condescending labels of *culture,* which they saw as standing in for a proxy for irrationality. They sought to challenge neocolonial narratives that dehumanized immigrants and non-White cultures in the West. They focused on bringing to the fore what they considered to be the crucial role played by colonial discourse within the multifaceted technologies of rule. Concepts such as 'epistemic violence' sought to highlight the importance of this discourse and its construction of the Global South as the 'Others' of the racially superior West. Foucault's work on the relationship between knowledge and power proved invaluable to this new scholarship as it laid bare the ways in which colonial rule was established, legitimated, and reproduced across the world. The Eurocentrism of mainstream theory within the humanities and social sciences was challenged, and extant explanations about 'backward' societies upended. A new set of theoretical and methodological tools were developed to challenge the colonial tropes and frames, which continued to define, categorize, and 'save' the natives who could not be trusted to do the job themselves despite their political independence (see Ashcroft, Griffiths, & Tiffin, 2006). Postcolonial scholarship began to emerge in a variety of disciplines, including sociology (Bhambra, 2007), anthropology (Clifford, 1994), psychology (Hook, 2005), and economics (Zein-Elabdin & Charusheela, 2004).

The idea of postcoloniality emerged into management theory in the late 1990s (Prasad, 1997a). Of course, this moment had its prehistory as well, which includes critiques of Eurocentrism in international management research (Boyacigiller & Adler, 1991), analyses of the silencing of minority women in academic texts (Calás, 1992), critiques of seemingly emancipatory discourses such as postmodernism from the perspective of poorer nations (Radhakrishnan, 1994), and attempts to theorize the culpability of global capital and multinational corporations (MNCs) in the furtherance of 'pre-modern atavisms' such as female feticide (Mir, Calás, & Smircich, 1995). But Prasad's article (which expanded on a 1994 conference paper) may have been the first journal publication in management theory that explicitly invoked postcolonial theory within the realm of organizational studies. Prasad (1997a,: 91) sought to interrogate "Europe's claim to universality as its problematic, and to contend that any serious attempt to reorganize the past and/or the future must subvert the European appropriation of the universal." In the same year, he also contributed a book chapter to an edited volume on organizational diversity, where he systematically laid out an overview of postcolonial theory in the organizational studies realm (Prasad, 1997b; see pp. 287–290).

In the two decades and more since, the postcolonial analytic has seen a significant expansion in the field of organizational studies. Despite the circumspect assertion by the editors of a recent special journal issue on postcolonialism that it is "still a somewhat quiet and tentative voice around the margins of orthodox MOS [management and organizational studies]" (Jack, Westwood, Srinivas, & Sardar, 2011: 275), an examination of the literature points to a flowering of sorts. It appears that postcolonial theory has been deployed in a variety of ways in organizational studies, as laid out in a number of publications (see Jack *et al.*, 2011: 279–280, Prasad, 2011: 29, and Banerjee & Prasad, 2009: 92–93).

In management theory, the three hegemonic postcolonial concepts that have been deployed most often are Orientalism, hybridity, and strategic essentialism. That is not to say that other ideas have not been invoked; for example, critical feminists have often deployed the work of postcolonial feminists like Chandra Mohanty in their work (Calás & Smircich, 1999), theorists working on an Africa-centered perspective have highlighted anti-colonial precursors of postcoloniality such as Senghor, Memmi and Nkrumah (Nkomo, 2011), while the researchers studying the psychological impacts of the colonial experience on organizational relations have made use of the work of Ashis Nandy, which provides a psychoanalytic component to the theorizing of knowledge from the South (Srinivas, 2012). In the interest of space however, we will confine our discussion to the concepts of Orientalism, hybridity, and strategic essentialism.

Orientalism

Edward Said himself was surprised by the success of his work, in which he had argued that the military and administrative conquest of the colonized nations by the Western powers was followed by a *discursive conquest*, whereby the 'Orient' was epistemically produced by the West, as alternatively naïve, rapacious, cruel exotic, and irrational. He saw Orientalism as "the corporate institution for dealing with the Orient – dealing with it by making statements about it, authorizing views of it, describing it, by teaching it, settling it, ruling over it: in short, Orientalism [was] a Western style for dominating, restructuring, and having authority over the Orient" (Said, 1978: 2).

Samuel Huntington's *clash of civilizations* argument, which sought to force cultural and religious frameworks on conflicts that were political in nature (Huntington, 1996), can be understood as an example of latter-day Orientalism insofar as it affirms a reductive essentialism. The phrase 'clash of civilizations' itself carried immense political baggage given that it was first used by the latter-day Orientalist Bernard Lewis in his influential article 'The roots of Muslim Rage' (Lewis, 1990). It was hardly surprising that Huntington used Lewis' work to argue, in essence that in the post-Cold War era 'Islam' had replaced communism as the existential threat to the West.

The analysis of Orientalism in management theory has typically followed two trajectories. The first has interrogated the ideological foundations of the sedimented practices and theories of organization that pose as modern and progressive but are in fact discriminatory, exclusionary, and racist. For example, Victorija Kalonaityte analyzed diversity management initiatives at a Swedish municipal school for adults. Her work provided "a conceptual framework based on postcolonial theory in order to theorize how an essentialist notion of national culture contributes to the construction of ethnical minorities as culturally inferior" (Kalonaityte, 2010: 31). Charlotte Echtner and Pushkala Prasad conducted an analysis of brochures representing different countries from the Global South. Their findings revealed three myths about representations of these countries: the myth of the unchanged, the myth of the unrestrained, and the myth of the uncivilized. Such myths reinforce an ontological difference between the Western nations and these countries/destinations (Echtner & Prasad, 2003). Bill Cooke analyzed a distinctive form of management, Development Administration and Management (DAM), that is applied to countries from the Global South, which have been selected as targets for 'modernization.' He contended that DAM is "complicit in neo-liberal World Bank interventions in the Third World" (Cooke, 2004: 603).

Works within the second trajectory have sought to highlight the various forms of resistance articulated/practiced by the subjects of imperialism themselves, thereby attempting to restore dignity to them. For example, a study of the knowledge transfer routines enacted in the Indian subsidiary of a US-based MNC sought to make sense of seemingly irrational behavior by local labor in order to present it as a legitimate form of workplace resistance (Mir, Banerjee, & Mir, 2008). Similarly, Gavin Jack and Robert Westwood (2006) made extensive use of the critical concepts and methodologies developed within postcolonial studies in the past two decades to develop counter-orientalist narratives in their analysis of international and cross-cultural management studies, while Shoaib ul-Haq and Robert Westwood (2012: 249) interrogated the epistemological premises of mainstream organizational studies, arguing that they exhibit a "continued cultural and intellectual imperialism which persists in constituting asymmetries, dependency relations, and inequities which occlude, marginalize and silence much of the Global South in general and Islam in particular."

Hybridity

Theorists like Homi Bhabha, Stuart Hall, and Nestor Garcia Canclini developed the concept of *hybridity*, a state of cultural non-belonging brought about by the colonial experience (Bhabha, 1994; Garcia Canclini, 2005; Hall, 1992). In his 1994 book *The Location of Culture*,

Bhabha shows how colonial subjects, through an enactment of hybridity, carve out spaces for themselves that are unavailable to the colonial masters and how forms of colonial hybridity produced anxiety within the ranks of the colonizer. Sometimes this hybridity is enacted through *mimicry*, a form of enactment of some of the rituals of the colonial power, but with a decidedly native touch.

Bhabha's ideas, while not as political as those of Fanon, nevertheless draw extensively on the latter's work, specifically his *Black Skin, White Masks*, in which Fanon articulated a powerful psychoanalytical critique of racialized colonialism and its effects on the colonized (especially members of the elite who were products of the kind of colonial strategy proposed by Macaulay in his Minute) based on his experience of being a Black intellectual in a White (French) world (Fanon, 1961). For Fanon, the liminal/hybrid condition of the colonized (elite) poses an existential problem for the latter. Bhabha, however, sees hybridity and mimicry as *camouflage*. Bhabha develops the idea of mimicry from the works of the French psychoanalyst Jacques Lacan, who sees mimicry as a coping mechanism for the vulnerable subject who is subject to intimidation:

> ...mimicry reveals something in so far as it is distinct from what might be called an *itself* that is behind. The effect of mimicry is camouflage, in the strictly technical sense [...] It is not a question of harmonizing with the background, but against a mottled background, of becoming mottled - exactly like the technique of camouflage practiced in human warfare.
>
> (Lacan, 1977: 99)

Bhabha suggests that aspects of colonial power are assimilated and appropriated by the colonial subject, thereby producing the possibility of subversion and resistance. A good example of this sense of hybridity/mimicry may be found in the game of cricket, which is currently far more popular in the erstwhile colonies of South Asia and the Caribbean than in England, where it originated. In his insightful book, *Beyond a Boundary*, the Trinidadian social theorist CLR James examines the tour of the West Indies cricket team (drawn from several Caribbean countries under the yoke of colonialism) and their experience of dealing constantly with issues of race, nationalism, and class. Offering a postcolonial/neo-Marxist analysis of the racial politics of cricket, James reads a desire for freedom exhibited by the manner in which the West Indians played the game. Unlike the British, who subjected the game to endless routines of decorum (including breaks in play for 'tea'), the Caribbean players played with fluid aggression, where the bowlers bowled to the body of the batsmen, the batsmen tried to whip the leather off the ball, all while watched by rambunctious supporters, with the sidelines characterized by impromptu reggae riff sessions. Mills notes that there was not merely prowess at play on the cricket field, but conflict, politics, and psychology as well (James, 1993).

Organizational theorists have used the concept of hybridity to move beyond the traditional binary of dominant versus oppressed and explore ways in which disempowered actors deploy hybridity and mimicry-based tools to carve out a space of agency for themselves. Michal Frenkel's study of international management discourse on knowledge transfer uses many of these concepts in analyzing an organizational setting (Frenkel, 2008). Pete Thomas and Jan Hewitt deploy critical discourse analysis to analyze professional organizations, a methodology developed by Chouliaraki and Fairclough (1999) using Bhabha's ideas along with those of theorists such as Ernesto Laclau and Chantal Mouffe (Laclau & Mouffe, 1985). They argue that managerialist discourse is "colonizing more aspects of contemporary life," and examine ways in which the power of this discourse was "mitigated by local circumstances, with local actors appropriating the discourse in ways that turned it to their advantage" (Thomas & Hewitt, 2011: 1379).

Strategic essentialism

In a 1988 article provocatively titled *Can the Subaltern Speak?* Gayatri Spivak continued the critique of European knowledge production about other parts of the world, in particular the Eurocentrism that presents Western ideas as objective and 'universal' principles (Spivak, 1988). She noted that this approach further disempowers those already oppressed by European domination, both past and present, both political and epistemological by rendering their subjectivities and experiences invisible. She illustrates this with reference to British colonial discourse on sati (or widow immolation) and draws a line from that to Foucault and Deleuze's declaration – based on the French student protests of 1967 – that representative politics had come to an end. Her answer to the question posed in the title of the essay is that the subaltern – and especially the poor Third World woman – cannot speak within the discursive frames of the West. These frames are designed to silence her, and replace her experience and subjectivity with that of the universal subject, the White European man.

One of Spivak's important contributions to postcolonial theory is the idea of 'strategic essentialism.' Spivak begins from the premise that essentialism – reducing diverse and unequal realities to some 'essential' truth – is dangerous from the point of view of progressive, liberatory politics. However, too much attention to difference can undermine the building of an effective political movement on behalf of a group (such as women). The posing of an essential identity (such as 'woman') as part of a political strategy of opposition/resistance to the status quo can thus serve a useful and necessary (but always limited) purpose. As articulated originally by Spivak, 'strategic essentialism' thus referred to a discursive political strategy employed by the subaltern group itself, a strategy that was always to be understood as limited in scope given the dangers inherent in essentialism.

The construct of strategic essentialism is especially malleable and can be applied to a variety of settings; to that extent it has traveled widely across disciplines, and occasionally has lost its critical edge. For instance, in the sociology/management literature, Paul McLaughlin has recently argued that the prescriptive claims made by *ecological modernization theory*, a methodology being deployed in the literature on environment sociology, is a form of strategic essentialism, which he broadens to define as "any attempt to use essentialist arguments and distinctions to manipulate the adaptive landscape(s) of one or more social roles, routines, or organizations" (McLaughlin, 2012: 190).

Examples of the use of strategic essentialism in critical organizational studies include Stella Nkomo's explicit invocation of her African identity in order to carve out an agential space for postcolonial as well as anti-colonial readings of 'African' leadership and management in organizational studies. In a 2011 article, Nkomo reports on her quest to find models of African leadership, and discovers that while Africa has been predictably marginalized in management discourse, the well-meaning responses by theorists to correct this imbalance "often unwittingly preserve, even as they attempt to overcome, the ideological coding of Western (primarily USA) conceptions of leadership and management" (Nkomo, 2011: 367). Nkomo attempts to infuse the ideas of postcolonial theorists with more political anti-colonial African theorists like Fanon, Césaire, and Senghor, to produce a narrative of Africa that recognizes both real-life struggles and representational issues. In her words,

> to fracture the dominant discourse, we must work in a third space if we wish to articulate alternative text(s) that transform not only the present representations of 'African' management and leadership but also the body of p. knowledge known as leadership and management in organizations.
>
> (Nkomo, 2011: 380)

We can see similar analyses in Marta Calás' attempt to represent Hispanic women in her critique of how they had been dealt with in organizational texts. She concludes that Latinas are mostly presented as docile and manually dexterous, making them good for factory work, but not so good for managerial and white-collar leadership tasks (Calás, 1992). Ajnesh Prasad has also used the concept of strategic essentialism as a way in which management scholars can move past "analytical categories of difference – whether they be based on gender, race, or sexual identity – in responding to issues of systemic inequalities in organizational life." In his formulation, strategic essentialism can be deployed in the field "as a means by which management scholars can tentatively engage with the research and the discourse that is reliant upon identity binaries, yet without reifying ideologically bifurcated identity classes" (Prasad, 2012: 567).

Neo-Gramscian philosophy: subaltern studies

In 1982, a group of Indian and English historians brought out the first of a series of volumes titled *Subaltern Studies* that attempted to correct the elitist nature of colonial historiography, which had written many of the subjects of colonialism out of its narrative (see Ludden, 2002 for a comprehensive review). Inspired in part by E.P. Thompson's magisterial 1963 book *The Making of the English Working Class* (Thompson, 2016), the group deployed Gramscian concepts towards an attempt to restore agency to the subjects of imperialism by reading official history 'against the grain.' The idea of subaltern historiography has since been expanded into a serious methodology, incorporating the theoretical insights of works such as James C. Scott's *Weapons of the Weak: Everyday Forms of Peasant Resistance* (Scott, 1985), Raymond Williams' *Marxism and Literature* (Williams, 1977), and the various critiques of Western scientific method examined by Gyan Prakash (1999) in *Another Reason: Science and the Imagination of Modern India*. The notion of subalternity was soon expanded beyond the frame of colonial historiography into a more generalized study of elite ideologies. The contention of subaltern theorists was that official accounts of resistance were contaminated with elitist bias, and a fine-grained account of the same phenomenon using a variety of textual sources could uncover and legitimize the perspective of the subaltern.

One of the early empirical studies of subaltern historiography was carried out in an organizational setting. In his 1989 book *Rethinking Working Class History,* Dipesh Chakrabarty attempted to write a history of jute-mill workers of Calcutta around the turn of the twentieth century. He began by using the tools of Marxist historiography, but layered them with hermeneutic analysis, Gramscian perspectives, and a documentary method in order to assert that his research uncovered "a capitalism that subsumes pre-capitalist relationships. Under certain conditions, the most feudal system of authority can survive at the heart of the most modern of factories" (Chakrabarty, 2000: xi). This is of course the reworking of an older Marxist idea, but Chakrabarty infuses his analysis with the use of a variety of cultural tropes that stand in for the labor-capital dialectic. In effect, Chakrabarty seeks to deploy newer tropes of class consciousness than the traditional Marxist ones, which he accuses of being derived from English conditions and imperfectly suited to India, where culture and consciousness have different meanings. For example, because of the social division of labor inherent in the caste system, Indian kinship relations have an economic component to them. Chakrabarty explicates this through his analysis, and offers ways to indigenize Marxist class analysis in the Indian context.

The survival, and even the furtherance of 'premodern atavisms' by global capital is extremely relevant to organizational studies. Consider, for example, the use of GE-made portable ultrasound machines in rural India to determine the sex of fetuses as a precursor to female feticide. The attempts by organizational theorists to study the impact of the entry of the MNCs into rural spaces hitherto somewhat removed from the dominant capitalist economy can be sharpened by the use of methods that have been developed by subaltern historiographers (Mir, Calás, & Smircich, 1995).

In his essay *Dominance Without Hegemony and Its Historiography*, Ranajit Guha (1989) provided one of the most powerful methodological applications of subaltern studies by proposing that the analytical category of hegemony as articulated by Gramsci was more theoretically useful and sophisticated than the mainstream Marxist understanding of ideology. Hegemony refers to the successful use of persuasion over coercion by dominant groups in order to seek the active *consent* of subordinate groups. Of course, coercion can never completely be abandoned, a fact that Gramsci captures in his metaphor of the 'iron fist in the velvet glove.' For Gramsci, the hegemonic project consists of a web of social relations, ideas, and practices. In effect, hegemony is *a particular condition of dominance* where persuasion *momentarily* outweighs coercion. The refusal of management to relinquish authoritarian modes of control, or refusal of workers to be coopted into a fiction of empowerment, marks a moment where hegemony fails, and is shown to be mere dominance. Deploying this perspective to understand knowledge transfer routines within a corporation, scholars have demonstrated how the subaltern subjects in the organizational relationship who were powerless to defend themselves against dominance nevertheless fought hegemony through subtle acts of resistance "that were of minor consequence in and of themselves, but collectively functioned as building blocks of a counter-hegemony that decentered the legitimacy of the corporation" (Mir & Mir, 2009: 109).

The use of the subaltern studies framework also abounds in fields such as marketing, where critical scholars have attempted to critique the attempts by agents of global capitalism to equate *freedom* with *consumption*, and chart the ways in which subaltern 'consumers' resist this interpellation (Varman & Vikas, 2007). However, within organizational studies, subaltern studies has perhaps been most extensively and creatively deployed in the study of the field of accounting, which has been read as both the language of imperialism and a counter-language of emancipation and resistance (Neu & Heincke, 2004). For example, in an empirical analysis of a Sri Lankan corporation, Chandana Alawattage and Danture Wickramasinghe set out to show how "accounting [becomes] a hegemonic technology through which subalterns become governable, exploited and manageable" (Alawattage & Wickramasinghe, 2009: 381). In the process, they also demonstrated the ways in which the subaltern groups they studied were able to use a different (and emancipatory) mode of accounting, which the authors propose as being "a process of social transcription through which the subalterns gain their agential capacity to write back to the structural conditions to which they are subjected" (p. 398). These processes would include accounting for domestic labor accrued through kinship relations, making macro adjustments for past acquisitions of land from small farmers through coercive means, renaming putative 'uncultivated lands' as community-owned spaces, and insisting on the power of worker groups to analyze, evaluate, and transform statements relating to accounting and governance.

An exemplar of critical realism: political society

In 2005, the social theorist Partha Chatterjee (one of the founders of the *Subaltern Studies* collective) published a book titled *Politics of the Governed* (Chatterjee, 2005a). Building on his earlier critique of nationalism (Chatterjee, 1992) where he had proposed that the dominant discourse of Indian nationalism was unable to accommodate certain subjectivities (the eponymous 'fragments' of the Nation), Chatterjee now argued that these subjectivities were also condemned to remain outside the purview of civil society. Chatterjee saw current institutions of civil society as little more than "the closed association of modern elite groups, sequestered from the wider popular life of the communities, walled up within enclaves of civic freedom and rational law" (Chatterjee, 2005a: 4). Within Chatterjee's framework, political society is a specific term (contrasted against 'civil society') that constitutes large sections of the fragments of the national community, who do not relate to the nation or the state in the same way that the elite and middle classes do. Drawing upon the Foucauldian field of governmentality studies, Chatterjee proposed a distinction between 'citizens' with rights and 'populations' who are targets of policies by the welfare state. However, the latter still make claims on the state, albeit through unstable arrangements arrived at through direct political negotiations. Political society is the realm of governmentality, of instrumental alliances between marginalized groups, and the attempts by populations whose very existence is beyond the pale of legality to wrest some concessions from the state. The struggles of undocumented immigrants in the USA to secure human rights for themselves in a context where they have no formal access to the Constitution represent the best possible example of political society in the West.

In a subsequent work titled *Lineages of Political Society*, Chatterjee elaborated his position through references to Foucault's idea of governmentality: "on the plane of governmentality, populations do not carry the ethical significance of citizenship" (Chatterjee, 2011: 14). This, he sees as an opportunity for the populace to engage in a collective struggle in order to wrest rights for themselves from institutions that may not see them as legitimate. To him, political society is a very empirical concept, invested with an immediacy that helps organizational researchers make sense of and theorize the action of corporations and capitalists all over the world. Chatterjee takes the issue of formulations such as those made by Hardt and Negri (2001) that new globalized networks of economic and cultural production have produced the conditions of possibility for a new immanent, deterritorialized and decentered Empire (Chatterjee, 2005b). Rather, he sees that spatial constraints remain relevant, especially for disadvantaged groups that are spatially tethered to a nation-state and simultaneously excluded from its ideological representation of its governmentality. The only recourse to democracy for such groups comes from "a network of norms in civil society that prevail independently of the state and are consistent with its laws" (Chatterjee, 2005a: 33).

The case of indigenous communities who live on lands that have been identified as mineral-rich is probably the most instructive for the purposes of organizational studies. These communities, despite having lived on their land for generations, do not possess formal property rights, and the state (in collusion with multinational mining companies) may slate them for eviction. In some cases governments have brazenly declared densely populated areas as 'uninhabited' in order to facilitate the commencement of mining operations by MNCs. The militant response of the displaced (or the 'to-be-displaced') populations represents an example of political society, and has led to organizational theorists developing a new theory of the 'translocal' (Banerjee, 2011).

The philosophical foundations of political society are predicated on ontological realism, a solidarity with the under-laborer that not only informs its politics but seeps into the epistemological domain, and locates its focus on the contingent relationships between phenomena and institutional structures. To that end, it represents a good example of critical realism as practiced in the organizational domain.

Critical management scholars have contended that concepts such as corporate social responsibility and corporate citizenship are ideological Trojan horses constructed by complicit theorists to indemnify corporations against peripheral stakeholders who may demand that they be compensated for the hardships heaped upon them by corporate activity. These concepts also help protect corporations from coming under the oversight of states, should the latter attempt to regulate their operations or tax them more in the interest of other social groups.

As neoliberalism intensifies and more and more of the world's people are left politically and socially marginalized in its wake, political society represents a significant counterweight to corporate power. It may also present a much-needed and useful theoretical frame since

> we need ... theories to understand why South Korean farmers picket the WTO in Hong Kong, Nigerians disrupt Shell corporation, French farmers attack McDonalds, or US citizens [picket mortgage brokers].... Political society represents the last and latest effort of the fragments to assert themselves against the hegemonic dominance of the state *and* civil society by corporations, and we as organizational theorists will ignore it at our own peril.
> (Mir, Marens, & Mir, 2009: 852)

The creative resistance practiced by the indigenous Zapatista movement in the Chiapas region of Southern Mexico has similarly informed a variety of work within organizational theory (e.g. McGreal, 2013). Likewise, we can consider an ethnographic study of undocumented workers and activists in the Chicago area where the authors re-theorized the rights of undocumented immigrants within the frame of labor rights. They highlighted how widespread economic insecurities that are the hallmark of neoliberal economic policies led to a wave of anti-immigrant emotions among the mainstream. At the same time, they produced clear examples of "the apparent hypocrisy of policies that allow for widespread consumption of their labor and tax dollars while denying them access to rights" (Gomberg-Munoz & Nussbaum-Barberena, 2011: 374).

One anticipates that the relatively new concept of political society will gain greater traction in the management realm in the next few years, especially as more and more of the instances of resistance to multinational capital and neoliberal development strategies seem to be falling along these lines. We suggest that using the lens of political society might have two productive effects. First, it would help us *theorize* workers struggles rather than *anthropologize* them. In other words, we must assume a logic to their actions, and not fetishize them as opaque cultural practices. For example, Aihwa Ong, writing in 1987, had theorized the periodic seizures and 'spirit possessions' suffered by Malay women working on the shop floors of modern factories as a form of resistance to capitalist discipline (Ong, 1987). The everyday relations at global workplaces have to be seen as sites of class struggle, of worker alienation, of intra-organizational bargaining, and sometimes, of relations of imperialism and cultural dislocation, whatever their context. Second, as indigenous people all over the world begin to struggle against corporations that seek to displace them in the name of industrial growth (Banerjee, 2011) or exploit them in the name of bottom-of-pyramid strategies (Prahalad, 2005), the use of a political society lens through which to view these struggles will help us see and thereby foreground their similarities and see them as part of the same problematic rather than as separate and bounded struggles.

Reflexive ontology: the case of critical transnationalism

The transnational turn in social theory may be seen as an attempt to decenter the tendency to fetishize the nation-state as the only valid unit of analysis. Not only is the nation-state a relatively recent construct which has never really been as bounded an entity as it was imagined to be, global capitalism has effectively undermined whatever stability it had in territorial and cultural terms (Castells, 2009). The cumulative effect of new forms of communication and networking, and of the fluidity and speed of global capital has been the emergence of new organizing arrangements, along with increasingly hybrid and fluid identities (Vertovec, 2009).

However, unlike most analyses of globalization and transnationalism which tend to be celebratory in one way or another, our concern here is with the critical approaches (see Schiller & Faist, 2010 for a review), especially those that deal with issues of the global labor force. In his analysis of the relationship between globalization and labor, Ronaldo Munck (2002) had suggested that the new era of globalization represents a second "great transformation," along the lines of the one ushered in by the industrial revolution and theorized by Karl Polanyi (1957). Munck identified two elements of this transformation as they relate to labor. The first, 'deterritorialization,' is produced by the tendencies of capital to free itself from the constraints of geographic space. Karl Marx had referred to this concept in his 1858 opus *Grundrisse* as the "annihilation of space by time" (Marx, 1993: 538), and indeed it appears that through a variety of maneuvers, MNCs have now rendered space less important (though never irrelevant) for the purposes of economic advantage. The second tendency created by globalization is 'Brazilianization,' or the spread of Third World-like work patterns into the industrial North. Increasingly we are seeing the emergence of a contingent labor economy in the industrialized rich nations, where temporary and precarious work is becoming more and more prevalent. In effect, the privileged position of First World labor vis-à-vis labor in the Third World has now been eroded by the ability of multinational capital to exploit the cheapest labor across the world.

The issue of the economic mobility of the MNCs raises some thorny sidebar issues about international governance. In particular, Western corporations have often sought to develop the regime of corporate social responsibility as a voluntaristic, internally driven, unsupervised 'civil society' initiative to align corporate interests with broader social interests (Marens, 2010). This may backfire, as it did in the case of the child labor controversy that affected the Pakistani soccer ball industry. By focusing on child labor without analyzing issues of poverty and wages, Western corporations and NGOs inadvertently caused harm to the general economic well-being of the most marginal of Pakistani workers, where family labor had become the last refuge against starvation (Khan, Munir, & Willmott, 2007), thereby demonstrating the ineffectiveness of international CSR regimes (similar critiques can be made of regimes such as the UN Global Compact, as well as voluntary codes by companies such as Nike and Apple). In brief, nationally anchored modes of governance have worked more effectively at reining in corporate excesses than transnational regimes, which are often predisposed to use universal models that pay less attention to context, and are susceptible to manipulation by dominant capitalist actors.

Various organizational theorists dealing with the MNCs have incorporated issues of transnationalism into their analytic framework (see Metcalfe & Woodhams, 2012: 132–134 for a review on how transnationalism has been deployed in organizational studies). Glenn Morgan (2001: 127), in his analysis of transnational communities and business systems, asked for research that could "shed light on the degree to which [MNCs] are simple extensions of national practices to an international level, or are in fact new forms of transnational communities," and management scholars have responded positively to such calls. For example, through an ethnographic analysis of an MNC, Galit Ailon and Gideon Kunda reached the conclusion that MNCs needed to be studied not just as economic entities but also as powerful ideological actors who imposed their own cultural regimes on their constituents. Ailon and Kunda (2009: 693) contend that

> this regime lays foundations for a transnational 'imagined community' which does not rival the national one, but internalizes it, creating an arena of discretionary power for managers: deciding when to activate and when to suppress nationality in the global organizational universe.

In effect, historical imbalances of power (such as those experienced in the Israel-Palestine context, or a difference in the economic power of different countries) end up rendering MNC culture ethnocentric, thereby undercutting the claims of global corporations that they are transcending national boundaries by becoming transnational (Boussebaa, Morgan, & Sturdy, 2012).

From a philosophical standpoint, one could consider critical nationalism as a realist perspective. What sets it apart though is its advocacy of reflexivity on the part of the researcher of transnationalism, not just at the epistemological level but also at the level of ontology itself. Reflexivity is engendered by the researcher through self-reference. The tension between self-reference on the part of the researcher and the sociological pulls of epistemic reflexivity is solved by recourse to ontological reflexivity (Bouzanis, 2017) that imbues critical nationalism with a philosophical uniqueness relative to other positions we have examined in this chapter.

Critical transnationalism has a very important role to play in organizational studies, and there are three points that must be kept in mind by scholars. First, a critical approach to transnationalism must begin with an acknowledgment of the uneven nature of globalization, especially as social and economic arrangements are transformed by the power of global capital. For example, one can chart a direct series of links between the global economic crisis that began in 2008 and a decline in the earning power of the poorest of trash-pickers in Mumbai (Boo, 2012). Likewise, one person's experience of the liberation associated with global consumption must necessarily be contrasted with another subject's experience of super-exploitation. Second, and following from this, national/regional/ethnic identity is no longer a useful category through which to understand the experience of the global workforce. As Mir, Mir and Ming-ji (2006: 168) contend, "even in relatively similar identity groups living and working in geographic proximity, there are workers (South Asian immigrant taxi drivers) and workers (South Asian immigrant stockbrokers), each with very different experiences of their work and their careers." Finally, a critical transnationalism must begin with the understanding that the category of economic class continues to be fundamental in any analysis of the relations of production, no matter how global they become. In the sub-zero sum game that characterizes the shrinking global economy, the apportioning of the benefits and suffering are heterogeneous and class-based. In their analysis of the 2008 economic crisis, Glenn Morgan, Julie Froud, Sigrid Quack, and Marc Schneiberg (2011) critique the way in which the crisis has morphed from a problem with capitalism into a statist fiscal crisis. In the words of their ringing critique,

> the blame game has shifted; in this discourse, the economic crisis is no longer the fault of the bankers but the consequence of an overly large and uncontrollable state, personified by welfare claimants and service users. It is these groups who must now pay the price of getting the economic system moving again by losing benefits, by working longer, by taking lower paid jobs, by accepting a decline in educational and health standards.
> (Morgan *et al.*, 2011: 148)

What we need today is an extension of the intersectional analysis of the kind first proposed by African-American feminist scholar Kimberle Crenshaw, which seeks to understand the complex and overdetermined way in which different aspects of social stratification intersect with each to produce the individual experience (Crenshaw, 1989).

One last important critical transnational perspective in management also involves theorizing 'south-south' dynamics such as the growing ties between Chinese corporations and African countries (Jackson, 2012). From a critical transnational perspective, the increasing presence of migrants, refugees, multi-ethnic identifications, and 'borderlands' in the global landscape has made critical transnationalism a crucial lens through which to examine organizational theory. For example, scholars who seek to study workplace diversity seriously will have to deal with issues such as outsourcing (Clott, 2004), migration (Mir, Mathew & Mir, 2000), international legal constraints (Hu, 2004), refugees (Keane 2004), and, within the realm of theory, the rapid unraveling of the dominant discourses of globalization (Banerjee & Linstead, 2001).

Conclusion

The past four decades have seen a massive uptick in the levels of inequality all over the world. Coinciding with the presidency of Ronald Reagan in the USA, the prime ministership of Margaret Thatcher in the UK, and other changes in the global leadership structure, institutions and nation-states have embarked upon macroeconomic policies that have reduced the footprint of the state on the global economy, intensifying regimes of privatization. This has been accompanied by large-scale deregulation that has created a climate crisis that threatens the world at a hitherto unknown scale. MNCs, dispersed as they are in space, have become skilled at the art of pitting nation-states against each other in the pursuit of foreign direct investments, to the point where they allow these firms latitude to pollute and exploit at a hitherto unacceptable rate. The fast moving circuits of financial capital preempt any attempts by nation-states to enact laws against global companies. Multilateral institutions like the World Trade Organization equalize international laws to suit firms at the expense of any state-level barriers to global capital. The emergence of the global supply chain has been facilitated by reduced worker protections, hostility towards collective action by labor, and the corralling of vast sections of the press by corporate interests. The result has been an emergent new world order that is hostile to the idea of equality, believing that 'growth' is the answer to the economic problems of the world, even if it produces greater inequalities and burns through natural resources, and that all attempts to resist this paradigm are fundamentally illegitimate, beholden as they are to failed relics of the past such as 'communism.'

Joining the policy makers and the press in this endeavor are groups of economists, theorists, and philosophers of various stripes and affiliated with various social sciences, whose job it is to ideologically legitimize the status quo and discredit those who resist it. In the eyes of such theorists, the interests of the elites can be extrapolated to the interests of the whole. In the field of organizational studies the primary assumptions appear to be that managers (should) speak for owners, and what is good for the owners is good for the business and is good for society. The normative interests of the sectional group, i.e. the top sliver, are represented as the universal interests of the organization. Adversarial action by any stakeholder group (employees, contractors, government, citizenry, regulatory institutions, or even specific customers/suppliers) can be bracketed away as 'resistance to change' or 'cultural conflict.' The mainstream theoretical apparatus works fundamentally by reducing the space for argument, and recasting the premises of the debate such that the points of contention are accorded the axiomatic status of the premises that underlie the argument, and therefore beyond debate. To that extent, organizational philosophy is often rendered functionalist, positivist, and status-quoist, bestowing the imprimatur of legitimacy on organizational action.

The paradigm shifts in organizational technologies have contributed to make the philosophical issues that underlie organizational action even more fraught than before. In a world that is now dominated by large information-intensive organizations that practice surveillance capitalism (Zuboff, 2019), the absence of any regulatory counterweight is proving deadly. The corporations that own these platforms have rendered themselves immune from legal oversight, and continue to further philosophical positions that imply that such a system is, on the one hand, inexorable and, on the other hand, benign and playful (Wittkower, 2010). The reality of course is far more severe; illiberal governments and their gangster proxies have used platforms such as Facebook and YouTube to wreak terror and violence against ethnic, religious, and sexual minorities (Stevenson, 2018).

In this chapter, we offer the counter-narrative to the philosophical business-as-usual perspective, opening up those very premises, and asking the very questions that the mainstreams of organizational philosophy have positioned as untouchable. 'Philosophy from below' is premised on a variety of positions, of which we have highlighted six. First, we interrogate the claim that the interests of the top layer of a firm of society are the same as the interests of the firm/society as a unit. Such a question lends itself to a class-based analysis. The second question that we raise is how we can remove the default male referent from an analysis of populations such that the female subjectivity is accorded autonomy and equality. Feminist analyzing provides an answer to this question. Our third question concerns the colonial/postcolonial subject, and asks whether those who had suffered under the economic and epistemic yoke of colonialism could reimagine their subjectivity in a manner that was no longer derivative. In a similar vein, our fourth question asked if cultural practices of the economic periphery could be visualized as autonomous and not tethered to a global economic base, such that the 'subaltern' subject could deny the elite their hegemony over the entire system. Our fifth question concerned political society, and asked how those subjects who were beyond the protections offered by the modern state (undocumented immigrants, non-employees) could find political agency for themselves through collective action. Our final question concerned the transnational subjects of the world, not just the jetsetters but refugees, economic migrants, those who were persecuted on account of their religious and ethnic identities and such, and how they could restore some dignity for themselves in the world.

'Philosophy from below' offers a variety of epistemological and methodological alternatives for those who seek to find dignity for the oppressed in an unequal world. Our choice of according this prominence in this book represents an ethical act, and fills an important hole in our theorizing.

Note

1 This chapter draws substantially (with permission) on formulations that were developed by Mir and Mir (2014).

References

Acker, J. (2006). Inequality regimes: Gender, class, and race in organizations. *Gender & Society, 20*(4), 441–464.
Ailon, G., & Kunda, G. (2009). 'The one-company approach': Transnationalism in an Israeli–Palestinian subsidiary of a multinational corporation. *Organization Studies, 30*(7), 693–712.
Alawattage, C & Wickramasinghe, D. (2009). Weapons of the weak: Subalterns' emancipatory accounting in Ceylon Tea. *Accounting, Auditing & Accountability Journal 22*(3), 379–404.
Althusser, L. (1965/2005). *For Marx* (Vol. 2). London: Verso.
Ashcroft, B., Griffiths, G. & Tiffin, H. (2006). *The postcolonial studies reader*. Abingdon: Routledge.
Balibar, É. (2014). *La philosophie de Marx*. Paris: La Découverte.
Banerjee, S. B. (2011). Voices of the governed: Towards a theory of the translocal, *Organization, 18*(3), 323–344.
Banerjee, S. B. & Linstead, S. (2001). Globalization, multiculturalism and other fictions: Colonialism for the new millennium? *Organization, 8*(4), 683–722.
Banerjee, S. B. & Prasad, A. (2009). Critical reflections on management and organization studies: A postcolonial perspective, *Critical Perspectives on International Business 4*(2/3), 90–98.
Benhabib, S. (1995). *Feminist contentions: A philosophical exchange*. London: Routledge.

Benson, J. K. (1977). Organizations: A dialectical view. *Administrative Science Quarterly*, *1*(1), 1–21.
Bhabha, H. (1984). Of mimicry and man: The ambivalence of colonial discourse, *Discipleship*, *28*(2), 125–133.
Bhabha, H. (1994). *The location of culture*. London: Routledge.
Boo, K. (2012). *Behind the beautiful forevers: Life, death, and hope in a Mumbai undercity*. New York. Random House.
Boussebaa, M. Morgan, G. & Sturdy, A. (2012). Constructing global firms? National, transnational and neocolonial effects in international management consultancies. *Organization Studies*, *33*(4), 465–486.
Bouzanis C. (2017). For reflexivity as an epistemic criterion of ontological coherence and virtuous social theorizing. *History of the Human Sciences*. *30*(5), 125–146.
Boyacigiller, N. & Adler, N. (1991). The parochial dinosaur: Organization science in a global context. *Academy of Management Review*, *16*, 262–290.
Braverman, H. (1974). *Labor and monopoly capital*. New York: Monthly Review.
Burawoy, M. (1979). The anthropology of industrial work. *Annual Review of Anthropology*, *8*(1), 231–266.
Butler, J. (2011). *Bodies that matter: On the discursive limits of sex*. London: Routledge.
Calás, M. B. (1992). An/other silent voice? Representing "Hispanic woman" in organizational texts. In A. J. Mills & P. Tancred (Eds.), *Gendering organizational analysis* (pp. 201–221). Newbury Park, CA: Sage.
Calás, M. B. & Smircich, L. (1999). Past postmodernism? Reflections and tentative directions? *Academy of Management Review 24*, 649–71.
Calás, M. B., Smircich, L., & Holvino, E. (2014). Theorizing gender-and-organization. In S. Kumra, R. Simpson & R. Burke (Eds.), *The Oxford handbook of gender in organizations* (pp. 605–659). Oxford: Oxford University Press.
Castells, M. (2009). *Communication power*. Oxford: Oxford University Press.
Chakrabarty, D. (2000). *Rethinking working-class history: Bengal 1890–1940*. Princeton, NJ, Princeton University Press.
Chatterjee, P. (1992). *The nation and its fragments: Colonial and postcolonial histories*, Princeton, NJ: Princeton University Press.
Chatterjee, P. (2005a). *The politics of the governed: Reflections on popular politics in most of the world*, New Delhi: Permanent Black.
Chatterjee, P. (2005b). Empire and nation revisited: 50 years after Bandung. *Inter-Asia Cultural Studies*, *6*(4), 487–496.
Chatterjee, P. (2011). *Lineages of political society: Studies in postcolonial democracy*. New York: Columbia University Press.
Chouliaraki, L. & Fairclough, N. (1999). *Discourse in late modernity*. Edinburgh: Edinburgh University Press.
Clifford, J. (1994). Diasporas. Toward ethnographies of the future. *Cultural Anthropology*, *9*(3), 302–338.
Clott, C. (2004). Perspectives on global outsourcing and the changing nature of work. *Business and Society Review*, *109*(2), 153–170.

Cooke, B. (2004). The managing of the (Third) World. *Organization*, *11*(5), 603–629.

Crenshaw, K. (1989). Demarginalizing the intersection of race and sex: A black feminist critique of antidiscrimination doctrine, feminist theory and anti-racist politics. *University of Chicago Legal Forum*, *139*(1), 139–167.

Dar, S. & Cooke, B. (2008). *The new development management: Critiquing the dual modernization*. London: Zed Books.

De Beauvoir, S. (1957/1988). *The second sex*. New York: Random House.

Echtner, C. & Prasad, P. (2003). The context of Third World tourism marketing, *Annals of Tourism Research*, *30*(3), 660–82.

Escobar, A. (1995). *Encountering development: The making and unmaking of the Third World, 1945–1992*. Princeton, NJ: Princeton University Press.

Fanon, F. (1961). The Wretched of the Earth, tr. *Constance Farrington, preface by Jean–Paul Sartre*. New York: Grove Press.

Fanon, F. (1961/1967). *The wretched of the earth*. London: Penguin.

Ferguson, K. (1984). *The feminist case against bureaucracy*. Philadelphia: Temple University Press.

Frenkel, M. (2008). The multinational corporation as a third space: Rethinking international management discourse on knowledge transfer through Homi Bhabha. *Academy of Management Review*, *33*(4), 924–942.

Garcia Canclini N. (2005). *Hybrid cultures: Strategies for entering and leaving modernity*. Minneapolis: University of Minnesota Press.

Gibson-Graham, J. K. (1995). *The end of capitalism (as we knew it): A feminist critique of political economy*. Oxford: Blackwell.

Gilligan, C. (1982). *In a different voice*. Cambridge, MA: Harvard University Press.

Gomberg-Munoz, R., & Nussbaum-Barberena, L. (2011). Is immigration policy labor policy?: Immigration enforcement, undocumented workers, and the state. *Human Organization*, *70*(1), 366–375.

Gramsci, A. (1954/1992). *Selections from the prison notebooks (1929-35)*, ed. and trans. Quintin Hoare. New York: Geoffrey Nowell Smith.

Guha, R. (1989). Dominance without hegemony and its historiography. In R. Guha (Ed.), *Subaltern Studies VI: Writings on South Asian history and society* (pp. 210–309). Oxford: Oxford University Press.

Hall, S. (1992). The question of cultural identity. In S. Hall, D. Held & A. McGrew (Eds.), *Modernity and its futures* (pp. 274–316). Cambridge: Polity Press.

Hook, D. (2005). A critical psychology of the postcolonial. *Theory & Psychology*, *15*(4), 475–503.

Hu, J. (2004). The role of international law in the development of WTO law. *Journal of International Economic Law*. *7*(1), 143–156.

Huntington, S. (1996). *The clash of civilizations and the remaking of world order*. New York: Simon and Schuster.

Jack, G. Westwood, R. Srinivas, N. & Sardar, Z. (2011). Deepening, broadening and re-asserting a postcolonial interrogative space in organization studies, *Organization*, *18*(3), 275–302.

Jackson, T. (2012). Postcolonialism and organizational knowledge in the wake of China's presence in Africa: Interrogating South-South relations, *Organization, 19*(2), 181–204.

Kalonaityte, V. (2010). The case of vanishing borders: Theorizing diversity management as internal border control, *Organization 17*(1), 31–52.

Keane, D. (2004). The environmental causes and consequences of migration: A search for the meaning of 'environmental refugees.' *Georgetown International Environmental Law Review, 16*(2), 209–223.

Khan, F. Munir, K. & Willmott, H. (2007). A dark side of institutional entrepreneurship: Soccer balls, child labour and postcolonial impoverishment, *Organization Studies, 28*(7), 1055–1077.

Knights, D., & Willmott, H. (Eds.). (2016). *Labour process theory*. London: Springer.

Kramarae, C. (1992). Gender and dominance. *Annals of the International Communication Association, 15*(1), 469–474.

Lacan, J. (1977). *The four fundamental concepts of psychoanalysis*. London: Hogarth Press.

Laclau, E., & Mouffe, C. (1985). *Hegemony and socialist strategy: Towards a radical democratic politics*. London: Verso.

Lewis, B. (1990). The roots of Muslim rage. *The Atlantic Monthly, 266*(3), 47–60.

Loomba, A. (2007). *Colonialism/postcolonialism*. London: Routledge.

Ludden, D. (2002). *Reading subaltern studies: Critical histories, contested meanings, and the globalisation of South Asia*. London: Anthem Press.

Macaulay, T. (1835/1972). *T. B. Macaulay: Selected writings*. Chicago: The University of Chicago Press.

Makki, F. (2004). The empire of capital and the remaking of centre–periphery relations. *Third World Quarterly, 25*(1), 149–168.

Marens, R. (2010). Destroying the village to save it: Corporate social responsibility, labour relations, and the rise and fall of American hegemony. *Organization, 17*(6), 743–766.

Marens, R. & Mir, R. (2016). Marxism: A philosophical analysis of class conflict. In R. Mir, H. Willmott & M. Greenwood (Eds.), *Routledge companion to philosophy in organizational studies* (pp. 138–150). London: Routledge.

Marx, K. (1993). *Grundrisse: Foundations of the critique of political economy*. London: Penguin Books.

Marx, K. (1998). *The German ideology, including theses on Feuerbach and introduction to the critique of political economy*, Buffalo, NY: Prometheus Books.

Marx, K. (1865/2018). *Das Kapital: A critique of political economy*. London: H. Regnery.

McGreal, S. (2013). The Zapatista rebellion as postmodern revolution. *Tamara: Journal for Critical Organization Inquiry, 5*(1), 54–63.

McLaughlin, P. (2012). Ecological modernization in evolutionary perspective. *Organization & Environment. 25*(2), 178–196.

Metcalfe, B. & Woodhams, C. (2012). New directions in gender, diversity and organization theorizing: Re-imagining feminist post-colonialism,

transnationalism and geographies of power. *International Journal of Management Reviews*, *14*, 123–140.
Miliband, R. (1969). *The state in capitalist society.* New York: Basic Books.
Mir, R., Banerjee, S. & Mir, A. (2008). 'Hegemony and its discontents: A critical analysis of organizational knowledge transfer,' *Critical Perspectives on International Business*, *4*(2). 203–227.
Mir, R., Calás, M. & Smircich, L. (1995). Global technoscapes and silent voices: Challenges to theorizing global cooperation. Paper presented at Case Western University in the conference titled *Organizational dimensions of global change*. Published in 1999 in David Cooperrider & Jane Dutton (Eds.) *Organizational dimensions of global change* (pp. 270–290). London: Sage Publications.
Mir, R. & Mir, A. (2009). 'From the corporation to the colony: Studying knowledge transfer across international boundaries,' *Group and Organization Management*, *34*(1), 90–113.
Mir, R. & Mir, A. (2014). Organizational studies and the subjects of imperialism. In P. Adler, G. Morgan & P. Du Gay (Eds.), *The Oxford handbook of sociology, social theory and organization studies: Contemporary currents* (pp. 660–683). Oxford: Oxford University Press.
Mir, R., Marens, R. & Mir, A. (2009). The corporation and its fragments: Corporate citizenship and the legacies of imperialism. In A. Scherer & G. Palazzo (Eds.), *The handbook of corporate citizenship* (pp. 819–852). London: Edward Elgar Press.
Mir, R., Mir, A. & Ming-Ji, D. (2006). 'Diversity: The cultural logic of global capital?' In A. Konrad, P. Prasad & J. Pringle (Eds.), *Handbook of workplace diversity* (pp. 167–188). London: Sage.
Mohanty, C. (1988). Under Western eyes: Feminist scholarship and colonial discourses, *Boundary 2*(3), 333–358.
Morgan, G. (2001). Transnational communities and business systems. *Global Networks 1/2*, 113–130.
Morgan, G. Froud, J. Quack, S. & Schneiberg, M. (2011). Capitalism in crisis: Organizational perspectives. *Organization*, *18*(2), 147–152.
Munck, R. (2002). *Globalisation and labour: The new great transformation.* London: Zed Books.
Nandy, A. (1983). *The intimate enemy: Loss and recovery of self under colonialism.* Delhi: Oxford University Press.
Neu, D. & Heincke, M. (2004). The subaltern speaks: Financial relations and the limits of governmentality, *Critical Perspectives on Accounting*, *15*(1), 179–206.
Nkomo, S. M. (2011). A postcolonial and anti-colonial reading of 'African' leadership and management in organization studies: Tensions, contradictions and possibilities. *Organization*, *18*(3), 365–386.
Ong, A. (1987), *Spirits of resistance and capitalist discipline: Factory women in Malaysia*, Berkeley: University of California Press.
Polanyi, K. (1957) The great *t*ransformation. Boston: Beacon Press.

Prahalad, C. K. (2005). *The fortune at the bottom of the pyramid: Eradicating poverty through profits*, New Delhi: Pearson Publishing.

Prakash, G. (1999). *Another reason: Science and the imagination of modern India*. Princeton, NJ: Princeton University Press.

Prasad, A. (1997a). Provincializing Europe: Towards a post-colonial reconstruction: A critique of Baconian science as the last strand of imperialism, *Studies in Cultures, Organizations and Societies 3*, 91–117.

Prasad, A. (1997b). The colonizing consciousness and representation of the other: A postcolonial critique of the discourse of oil. In P. Prasad, A. Mills, M. Elmes & A. Prasad (Eds.), *Managing the organizational melting pot: Dilemmas of workplace diversity* (pp. 285–311). Thousand Oaks, CA: Sage.

Prasad, A. (2003). *Postcolonial theory and organizational analysis: A critical engagement*. New York: Springer.

Prasad, A. (2011). Working against the grain: Beyond Eurocentrism in organization studies. In A. Prasad (Ed.), *Against the grain: Advances in postcolonial organization studies* (pp. 19–38). Copenhagen: Copenhagen Business School Press.

Prasad, A. (2012). Beyond analytical dichotomies. *Human Relations, 65*(5), 567–595.

Prasad, P. (2017). *Crafting qualitative research: Beyond positivist traditions*. London: Routledge.

Prichard, C. & Mir, R. (2010). Organizing value, *Organization, 17*(5), 507–515.

Radhakrishnan, R. (1994). Postmodernism and the rest of the world, *Organization, 1*(2), 305–340.

Rajan, B. (1999). *Under Western eyes: India from Milton to Macaulay*. Durham, NC: Duke University Press.

Said, E. (1978). *Orientalism*. New York: Pantheon.

Schiller, N. & Faist, T. (2010). *Immigration, development, and transnationalization: A critical stance*. Oxford: Berghahn Books.

Scott, J. (1985), *Weapons of the weak: Everyday forms of peasant resistance*, New Haven: Yale University Press.

Spivak, G. (1988). Can the subaltern speak? In C. Nelson & L. Grossberg (Eds.), *Marxism and the interpretation of culture* (pp. 271–313). Urbana: University of Illinois Press.

Srinivas, N. (2012). Epistemic and performative quests for authentic management in India, *Organization 19*(2), 145–158.

Stevenson, A. (2018). Facebook admits it was used to incite violence in Myanmar. *The New York Times, 6*.

Stone, K. (1974). The origins of job structures in the steel industry. *Review of Radical Political Economics, 6*(2), 113–173.

Thomas, P. & Hewitt, J. (2011). Managerial organization and professional autonomy: A discourse-based conceptualization. *Organization Studies 32*(10), 1373–1393.

Thompson, E. P. (2016). *The making of the English working class*. London: Open Road Media.

Ul-Haq, S. & Westwood, R. (2012). The politics of knowledge, epistemological occlusion and Islamic management and organization knowledge. *Organization, 19*(2), 229–257.

Valian, V. (1999). *Why so slow? The advancement of women.* Cambridge, MA: MIT Press.

Varman, R. & Vikas, R. (2007). Freedom and consumption: Toward conceptualizing systemic constraints for subaltern consumers in a capitalist society. *Consumption, Markets & Culture, 10*(2), 117–131.

Vertovec, S. (2009). *Transnationalism.* London: Routledge.

Williams, R. (1977). *Marxism and literature.* London: Oxford University Press.

Wittkower, D. E. (Ed.). (2010). *Facebook and philosophy: What's on your mind?* Chicago: Open Court.

Wollstonecraft, M. (1792/1992). A vindication of the rights of woman. 1792. *The Works of Mary Wollstonecraft, 5,* 79–266.

Zein-Elabdin, E. & Charusheela, S. (2004). *Postcolonialism meets economics.* London: Routledge.

Zuboff, S. (2019). *The age of surveillance capitalism: The fight for a human future at the new frontier of power.* New York: Profile Books.

4 The road ahead for management and organizational philosophy

In this book, we attempt to accomplish three very important things. To begin, in Chapter 1 *Everyone is a philosopher*, we offer a comprehensive introduction to philosophy that is accessible to all scholars. Our target audience is a student or early career researcher associated with a business school, but we believe that all levels of academics from a variety of disciplines, as well as interested professionals, can benefit from this introduction.

Moving from the introduction, in Chapter 2 *Interrogating concepts*, we analyze "concepts," which are the building blocks, not only of theory, but also of philosophy and method. Our argument here is that concepts could be deployed in a myriad of ways. Concepts can be thickened through a combination of homage and skepticism to build bridges between abstract theories and lived experiences. But concepts can also be thinned through reification and commodification, thereby entrapping the reader either in the rarefied amorphousness of grand theory or the reductive instrumentality of empiricism.

Our final discussion, Chapter 3 *Philosophy from below*, concerns the role of philosophers in analyzing the determinants of socio-economic inequality and exploitation. We offer an analysis of what we termed 'philosophy from below' as antecedent to action, whereby the principled researcher could advocate for those subjectivities who have been left behind by the dominant philosophical discourse as well as the institutions that promoted social safety.

The arguments we develop throughout the book are underpinned by a number of themes. First, we live with both philosophy and social science. Having argued that all knowledge inquiry invokes philosophy and philosophical thinking, and that the artificial separation between philosophy and social science is fallacious, we work with the tension between philosophy and social science throughout the book. Second, we confront the political. Just as philosophy is everywhere, so is power,

DOI: 10.4324/9781351030700-4

and for better or worse they go hand in hand. We do not shy from addressing the politics of our own research practice or the subjects of our inquiry. Third, philosophy is about taking action. The purpose of creating knowledge is to intervene in the world, to make it a better place.

We have one more message, encapsulated by the words of Umberto Eco (1994:24) "Pourquoi interpreter la confusion comme un malheur? [Why should we interpret confusion as a misfortune?]." Do not be concerned if you are confused, be concerned if you are not. Our world is so complex and changing that any certainty is likely to be at best fleeting, at worst false. As noted by Jones and ten Bos (2007: 3), "if we claim that organizations should be a philosophical subject, then it is because organization makes us anxious, curious, angry, hopeful, doubtful and confused." Ambiguity and puzzlement are starting points for philosophical inquiry.

What lies ahead then for organizational researchers who have familiarized themselves with the ideas contained in this book? We suggest that the best way forward is them to consider the specific ways in which they can incorporate philosophy into their own theoretical and empirical work. Drawing upon prior attempts by philosophically minded organizational theorists, we offer a list of topics where the philosophical foundations of research can be discussed and analyzed at length. We have derived this alphabetically ordered list from the different contributions made by our colleagues under the 'special topics' section of our edited book *The Routledge Companion to Philosophy in Organizational Studies* (Mir, Willmott, & Greenwood, 2016). The interested reader will find short chapters pointing them in important and useful directions in studying the philosophical foundations of these topics.

Whether one is studying *aesthetics and design* in organization or preconceptions associated with *aging*, the abstract ideas of *agency* or the corporeality of the *body* in organizations, the ephemeral world of marketing and *brands*, or the role of different forms of *capital* in the world of organizations, philosophy can help. Students of *commodification* and *consumption* can incorporate philosophy in their work, as can researchers analyzing the idea of shared labor, the *commons* and expropriation. Likewise, theories of *conflict* in organizations, of the modes of socio-organizational *control*, and of the governance mechanisms that turn organizations into *corporations*, are legitimate candidates for philosophical analysis.

Under regimes of capitalism, *debt* plays a significant role in the world of organizing. Likewise, *democracy* becomes a concept of great importance. The way in which *decision-making* occurs in organization and the roles played by *diversity* initiatives in organization lend themselves to issues of philosophizing. The relationship between firms and the *environment* provides a way to analyze and critique the discourse of extractivism that pervades corporate activity. The role played by *finance* in creating the capitalist ecosystem, as well as our approach to issues of *globalization*, begs a philosophical approach. The changing conceptions of the corporation can be better understood through a philosophical analysis of *governance,* while an understanding of *historiography* and the *historical* turn in organizational theory pulls us towards philosophical interdisciplinarity. On a lighter note, we can study *humor* in the workplace beyond the binary between the ludic and the critical, as a coping mechanism as well as an act of resistance.

The study of *identity* in organizational studies can proceed in many philosophical directions, as can an analysis of organizational *inequality* and the misery that can accrue (or be avoided) by firm actions. The role of *justice* in organizational practice as well as the much studied but rarely critiqued construct of *leadership* provides many a philosophical insight. *Management* is both a discipline and a mindset, and provides many avenues for philosophical analysis, as does the idea of *measurement*, which can analyze and critique the obsession with statistical analysis in our sub-fields. A philosophical analysis of *needs* in management theory and of the term *organization* itself takes us down the path of studying political theory. The different *paradigms* that animate organizational analysis are philosophies unto themselves, while the construct of *performativity* provides a philosophical linkage between ideas and praxis. *Power* of course is a perennial favorite of social theorists with a philosophical bent, while the study of *quantification* as a philosophical act links us back to our interrogation of measurement and statistics. As a corollary to the study of power, theorists can study the philosophical foundations of organizational *resistance*. Likewise, an anthropologically oriented organizational theorist could examine the philosophical basis of organizational *rituals.*

Spirituality and religion are an important element of organizational life, despite being less visible than its secular elements. *Strategy* of course is front and center, and hides many a philosophical conundrum behind its seemingly functionalist facade. The notion of organizational *trust* lends itself to critical reflection and scrutiny, while the idea of *value*, joined at the hip by the earlier idea of capital, offers many philosophical possibilities. The *visual* turn in organizational research offers newer philosophical ways of 'looking' at organizations, while the world of *work*, especially in this age of neoliberalism, demands philosophical introspection and analysis.

100 The road ahead for management philosophy

The listing of topics in this conclusion, while incomplete, is quite instructive.[1] It would be a lot easier to say that every topic in organizational research is ripe for philosophical analysis. We look forward to a thousand philosophical flowers blooming in the world of management and organizational research.

Note

1 This listing is a way for us to honor these friends and contributors to that section of the book: Antonio Strati, Kat Riach, Tracy Wilcox, Torkild Thanem, Adam Arvidsson, Harry Van Buren, Douglas Brownlie, Casper Hoedemaekers, Alessia Contu, Graham Sewell, Jeroen Veldman, Suhaib Riaz, Peter Edward, Phil Johnson, Joanne Duberley, Elaine Swan, Steffen Böhm, Maria Ceci Misoczky, Geoff Lightfoot, David Harvie, Guido Palazzo, André Spicer, Bobby Banerjee, Michael Rowlinson, Nick Butler, Kate Kenny, Nancy Harding, Hari Bapuji, Sandeep Mishra, Carl Rhodes, Jonathan Gosling, Peter Case, Campbell Jones, Michael Zyphur, Dean Pierides, Jon Roffe, Cristina Neesham, Martin Parker, John Hassard, Jean-Pascal Gond, Laure Cabantous, Stewart Clegg, Amit Nigam, Diana Trujillo, Carl Cederström, Gazi Islam, Emma Bell, Scott Taylor, David Levy, Reinhard Bachmann, Craig Prichard, Samantha Warren, and Peter Fleming along with a myriad of other friends who have shared philosophical insights with us.

References

Eco, U. (1994). *Six walks in the fictional woods*. Cambridge, MA: Harvard University Press.
Jones, C., & ten Bos, R. (2007). Introduction. In C. Jones & R. ten Bos (Eds.), *Philosophy and Organization* (pp. 1–17). Abingdon, Oxon: Routledge.

Index

academic knowledge production 20, 40–41, 45–47, 55; journals 45, 55 *see also* ethics: research ethics; postcolonial, postcolonialism: Eurocentrism
Academy of Management 2, 34, 52, 55
activism: academic 64, 68
actor-network theory 16
agency 17, 51, 56, 79
agency theory 13, 14–15 *see also* realism
Althusser, Louis 67–68 *see also* Marx, Karl: overdeterminism
ambiguity: ambivalence 36, 38, 47, 98

Bhabha, Homi 70, 75–77 *see also* Fanon, Frantz
Balibar, Etienne 66–67
Barthes, Roland 49; punctum 49
Bauman, Zygmunt 35–36
Bhaskar, Roy 14 *see also* critical realism
Black Skin, White Masks 76 *see also* Fanon, Frantz
Bourdieu, Pierre 43
Butler, Judith 56, 65

Can the Subaltern Speak? 77–78 *see also* Spivak, Gayatri
capitalism: global capital 73, 80–81, 84, 86–87; global labor 85; neoliberal 83–84 *see also* globalization

Chakrabarty, Dipesh 79–80
class conflict 64, 66–68
classification 35–37
concepts 31–58; commodification of 39–42, 44–45; 'conceptual leap' 50; definitions of 33–35; as gendered 68–69; as method 32, 46–48, 54–56; as thick 37–39; as thin 37–39, 42–43 *see also* constructs; qualitative methods
constructs: as compared with concepts 33–36; umbrella 40
constructivism 7, 15–16, 19, 23; critical 70–74 *see also* LaTour, Bruno
correlation 14
critical realism 7, 14–15, 19, 65
culture 43; cosmopolitanism 44; interculturalism 43–44
Culture's Consequences 43–44 *see also* Hofstede, Geert

de Beauvoir, Simone 68
definitions 5 *see also* values; ideologies
Deleuze, Gilles 32–33, 36, 39, 48–53; assemblages 52; *Body without Organs* 51; 'dogmatic image of thought' 48; haecceity 51
Dewey, John 16 *see also* pragmatism
Dominance Without Hegemony and its Historiography 80–81 *see also* Guha, Ranajit

Index

environmental crisis 4
epistemology 6–9, 19; epistemic decentering 65; epistemological decolonialization 71; epistemic violence 72; *see also* feminisms: feminist epistemologies
essentialism: essential truth 78 *see also* postcolonial, postcolonialism: strategic essentialism
ethics 6, 10–12, 20; institutional review 10–11, 55; research ethics 55 *see also* transparency
ethnography 15–16; critical ethnography 83–84, 86

fact-value distinction 16, 45, 58
falsifiability 3–4, 10, 13–14
Fanon, Franz 67, 71, 76, 78
feminisms 50, 65, 68–69; body 50; feminist epistemologies 69; liberal feminism; patriarchy 69; socialist feminism 69 *see also* concepts: as gendered; epistemologies: epistemic decentering; postcolonial, postcolonialism: feminism; queer theory: heteronormativity
Ferguson, Kathy 69
field: 48, 52–54; assemblages 52
Foucault, Michel 10, 32, 36, 38–39, 46, 72–73, 82
Fourier, Charles 68

gender 69; feminization 8; gender equality 68–69; *see also* feminisms; concepts: as gendered; queer theory
generalizability 3, 10, 14–15, 54; conceptual 37–38 *see also* concepts: as thick, as thin; positivism; qualitative methods; replication
global: Global South 65, 72 *see also* postcolonial; subaltern
globalization: global supply chain 88 ; globalized networks 82; transnationalism, transnational 85 *see also* capitalism
governance 20, 71, 85, 98–99
Gramsci, Antonio 65, 67, 79–81
Guha, Ranajit 79–81

habitus 43 *see also* Bourdieu, Pierre
Hawthorne studies 13
hermeneutics: of faith 38, 45–46; of skepticism 38, 45–46
Hofstede, Geert 43 *see also* culture

ideology 4–5, 15, 17, 19, 67–68
inequality 3–4, 17–18; *see also* gender: gender equality; postcolonialism; subaltern
institutional theory 6–7, 40

James, William 16 *see also* pragmatism
justice: 42–43; organizational 42

knowledge 73; knowability, understandable 70 *see also* Foucault, Michel

labor process theory 15, 67
Lacan, Jacques 76
language: of biology 40; of markets 40
Latour, Bruno 15–16

management consultant 39; interculturalist 43–45; trainers, training 44
Marx, Karl 20, 64, 66–67, 71; capitalism 66; class-based analysis 65; dialectic practice 67; economic determinism 67; Eleventh Thesis on Feuerbach 64; historical materialism 67; overdetermination 67–68; reflexivity versus realism 66 *see also* class conflict; globalization: global capital
methodology 6, 9, 19, 54–56
Mobius Strip 49–50, 58n8

Nietzsche, Friedrich 35–**36**, 38, 56, 58

objectivity 8, 17, 33–34, 51, 59n9, 77 *see also* observability; positivism; subjectivities
observability 12; unobservables 13–14
ontology 6–7, 9, 12, 19; concepts as 58; reflexive ontology 66, 84–88

paradigm 3, 12, 17, 99 *see also* constructivism; critical realism;

epistemology; ontology; positivism; realism
performance 47; organizational 43
performativity 20, 23–24n5., 31, 36, 42, 58n3., 99
political 12, 17–19, 40, 45–47; society 84
positivism 7, 12–13, 19, 21–22
postcolonial, postcolonialism 20, 65, 70–79; Critical Transnationalism 66, 84–88; development, development project 71; discursive conquest 74; Eurocentrism 73; hybridity 75, 76–77; modernity, modernization theory 71; Orientalism 72, 74–75; feminism 69, 74; paternalism 71; strategic essentialism 75, 77–79 see also epistemic violence; epistemological decolonization; political: society
post-modernism: post-modern condition 47
post-qualitative inquiry 46, 48–50, 55–56; post-humanist inquiry 48; refusal methodology 48
power 64, 73 see also knowledge; postcolonial: Eurocentrism
practice 7, 53
practice theory 16, 21
pragmatism 7, 12, 16–17, 19
psychoanalysis 69

qualitative methods 8, 10; 46–54; anti-method 47, 55; clinical cases 53–54; deconstruction 48; interview 48; observation 48 see also field; post-qualitative inquiry; concepts: conceptual leap; ethics: research ethics
queer theory 20, 65, 69; heteronormativity 65, 69

realism 7, 13–14, 19, 21
reflexivity 53–54; versus realism see also realism
reification 45, 57, 69; anti- 16
replication 13–14
representation 13
resistance 11, 64, 75, 76, 78, 79, 81, 83–84

resource-based view 13, 21 see also realism
Rethinking Working Class History 79–80 see also Chakrabarty, Dipesh
Ricoeur, Paul 33–**35**, 38, 42–43, 45

Said, Edward 72
Schutz, Alfred 33–**35**
social science 32–34, 43; theory 5, 19–21
Sociological Paradigms and Organizational Analysis 17, 54–55
Spivak, Gayatri 77–78
Stone, Katherine 67
strategy 14; strategic management 20–23
subaltern 64, 65 see also *Can the Subaltern Speak?*
subject-object relation 8 see also epistemology
subjectivities 15, 17, 32, 41, 47, 49, 51–53, 55–56, 65, 77; subjectification 47; human subjectivity 51; individual 'I' 51; marginalized 65; non-Western 65; universal subject 77 see also Deleuze, Gilles: *Body without Organs*; haeeceity

Taylor, Frederick 13
technologies, technological 7, 13; institutional 41, 89; of rule 72
The Location of Culture 75–76 see also Bhabha, Homi
The Origins of Job Structures in the Steel Industry 67 see also Stone, Katherine
The Radical Case Against Bureaucracy 69 see also Ferguson, Kathy
transaction cost economics 3–4, 13 see also realism
transparency 2, 6, 11–12, 20
truth; claims 3, 13 see also falsifiability; 'voice from nowhere'

values 2, 5, 8, 11, 42, 45; fact-value distinction 42, 58n2.; value-free 3–4, 42, 45
'voice from nowhere' 51, 59n9

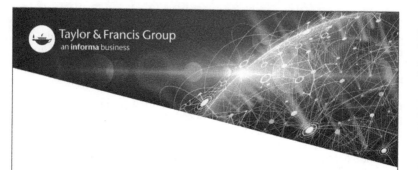